RUBY FALLS

BERGER BOOKS

AN IMPRINT OF
DARK HORSE COMICS

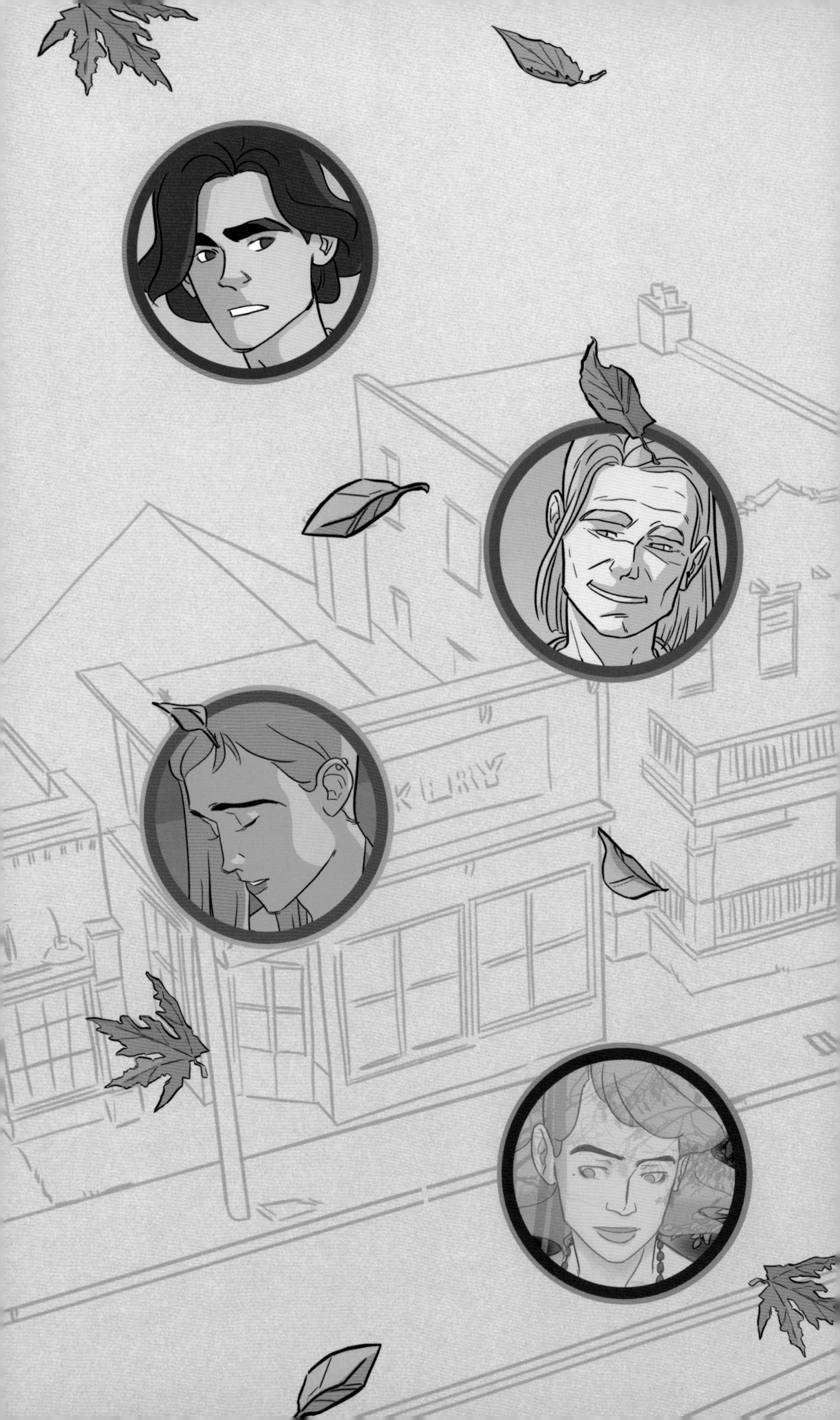

Ann Nocenti WRITER

Flavia Biondi ARTIST

Lee Loughridge COLORIST

Sal Cipriano LETTERER

Ruby Falls™

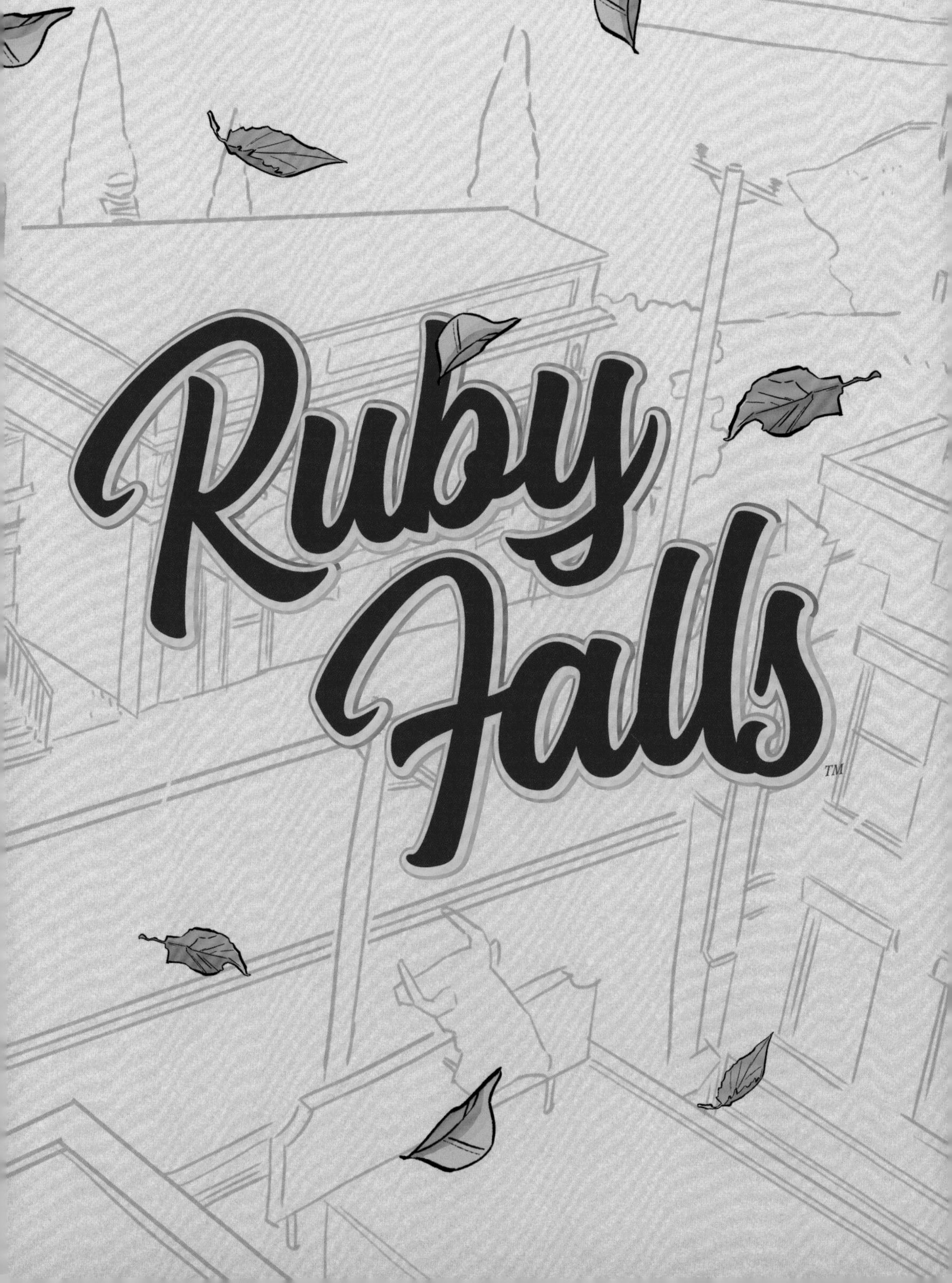

Karen Berger EDITOR

Rachel Boyadjis ASSISTANT EDITOR

Richard Bruning LOGO/BOOK DESIGN

Adam Pruett DIGITAL ART TECHNICIAN

Mike Richardson PRESIDENT & PUBLISHER

RUBY FALLS, April 2020. Published by Dark Horse Comics LLC, 10956 SE Main Street, Milwaukie, OR 97222. Text and illustrations of Ruby Falls™ © 2019 Ann Nocenti and Flavia Biondi. The Berger Books logo, Dark Horse Comics®, and the Dark Horse logo are registered trademarks of Dark Horse Comics LLC, registered in various categories and countries. Berger Books® is a registered trademark of Karen Berger. All rights reserved. No portion of this publication may be reproduced or transmitted, in any form or by any means, without the express written permission of Dark Horse Comics LLC. Names, characters, places, and incidents featured in this publication either are the product of the author's imagination or are used fictitiously. Any resemblance to actual persons (living or dead), events, institutions, or locales, without satiric intent, is coincidental. Printed in Canada.

This volume collects Issues #1-4 of *Ruby Falls.*

First Edition: April 2020
ISBN 978-1-50671-495-0

Digital ISBN 978-1-50671-490-5

1 3 5 7 9 10 8 6 4 2

Printed in China

Published by
Dark Horse Books
A division of Dark Horse Comics LLC
10956 SE Main Street, Milwaukie, OR 97222

DarkHorse.com
ComicShopLocator.com

Names: Nocenti, Ann, author. | Flavia, Biondi, artist. | Loughridge, Lee, colorist. | Cipriano, Sal, letterer.
Title: Ruby Falls / script, Ann Nocenti ; art, Biondi Flavia ; colors, Lee Loughridge ; letters, Sal Cipriano.
Description: First edition. | Milwaukie, OR : Berger Books : Dark Horse Books, 2020. | "This volume collects Issues #1-4 of Ruby Falls."
| Identifiers: LCCN 2019054144 | ISBN 9781506714950 (trade paperback) | ISBN 9781506714905 (ebook) Subjects: LCSH: Comic books, strips, etc. | Classification: LCC PN6728.R8 N63 2020 | DDC 741.5/973--dc23
LC record available at https://lccn.loc.gov/2019054144

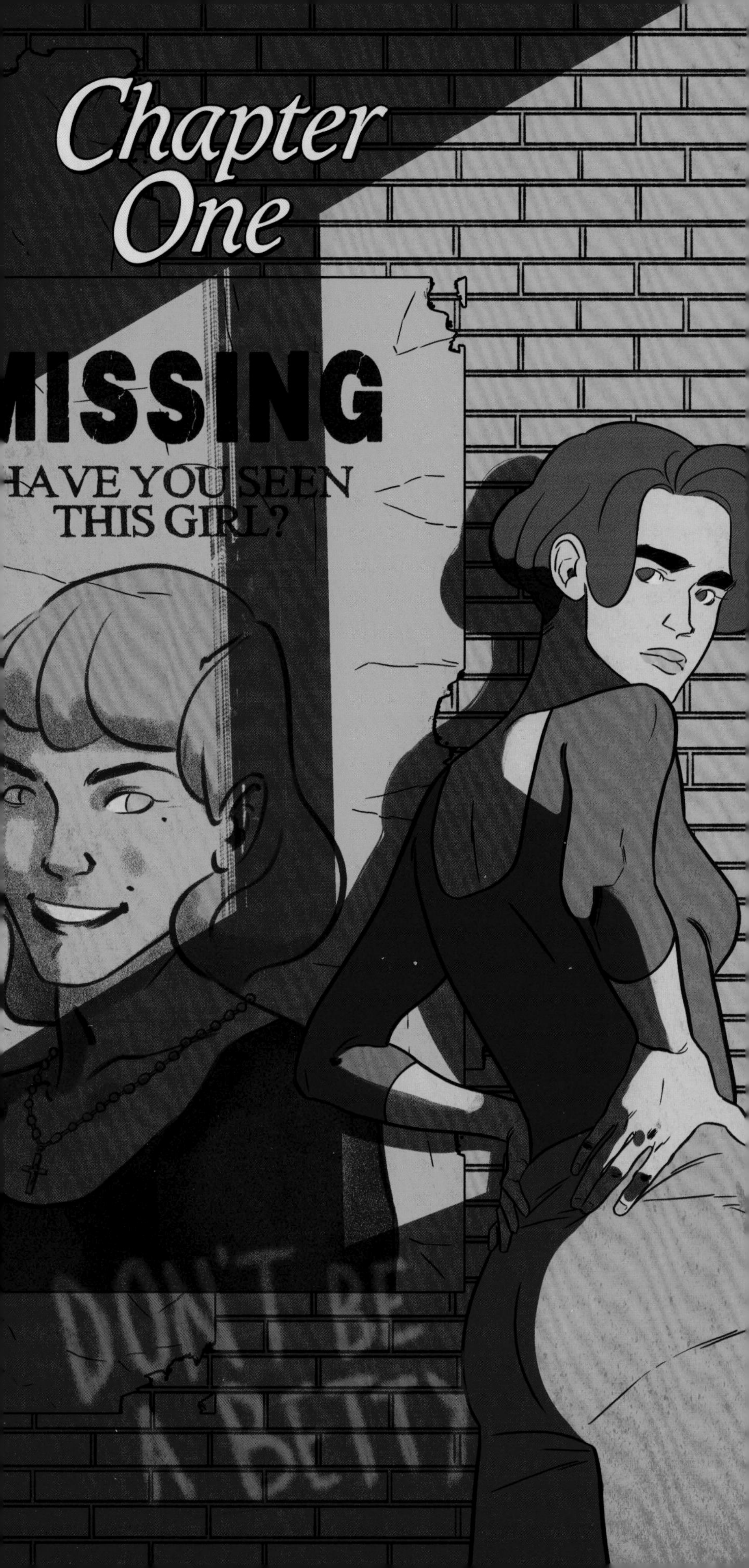

Chapter One
MISSING
HAVE YOU SEEN THIS GIRL?
DON'T BE A BETTY

❝ *A clear conscience*

is the sure sign

of a bad memory. **❞**

~**MARK TWAIN**

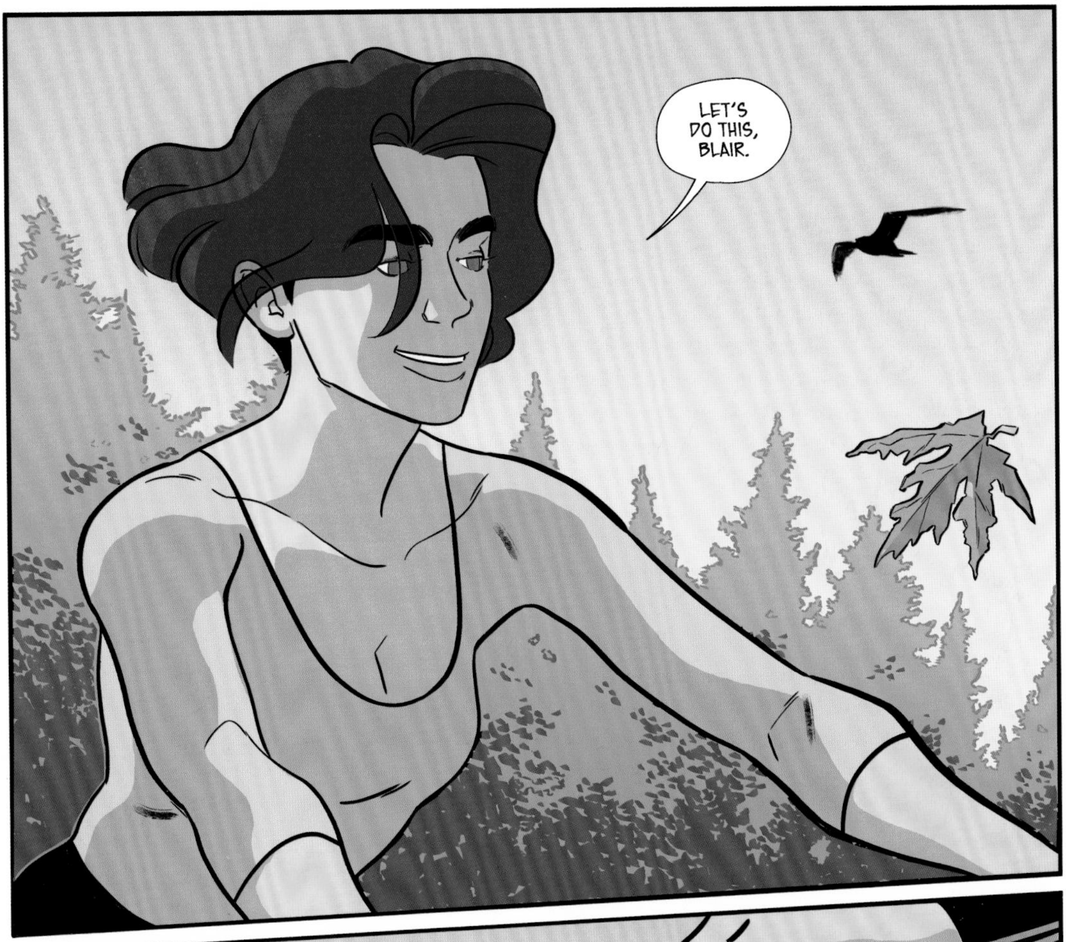
LET'S DO THIS, BLAIR.

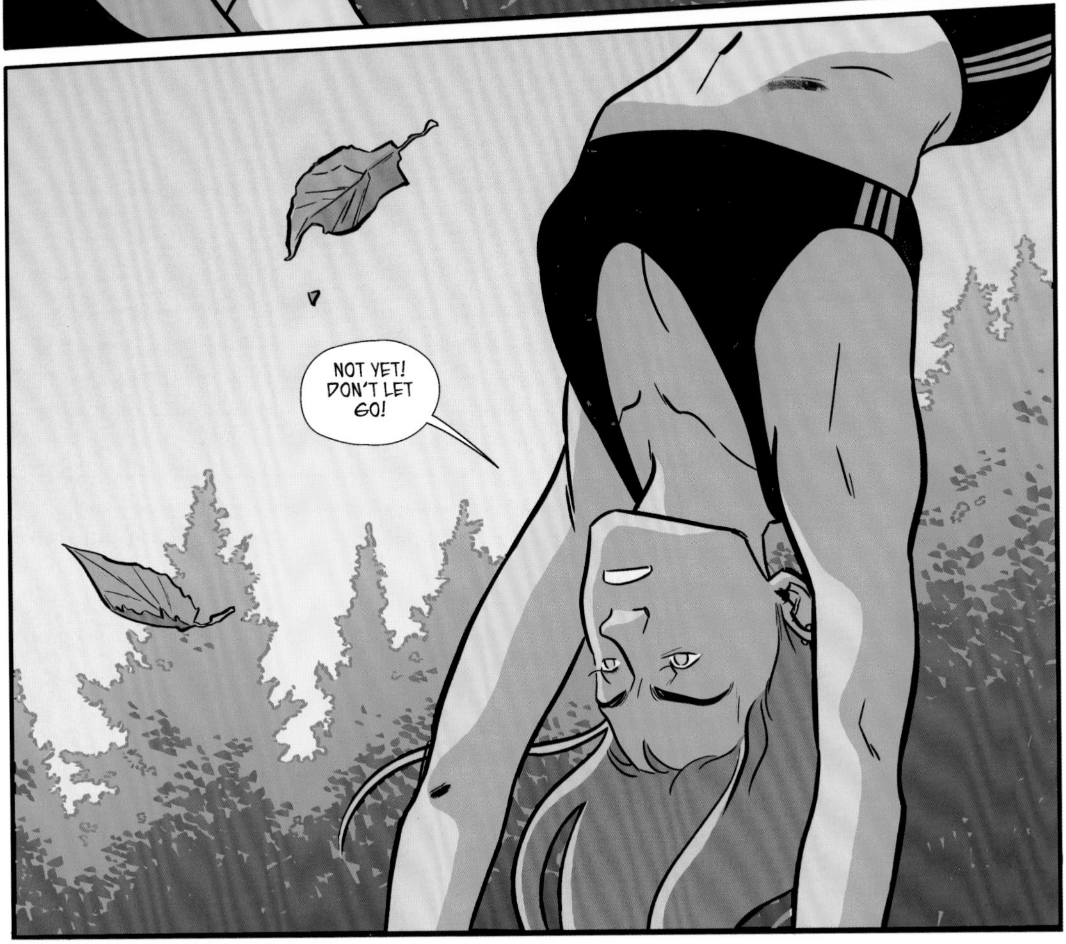
NOT YET! DON'T LET GO!

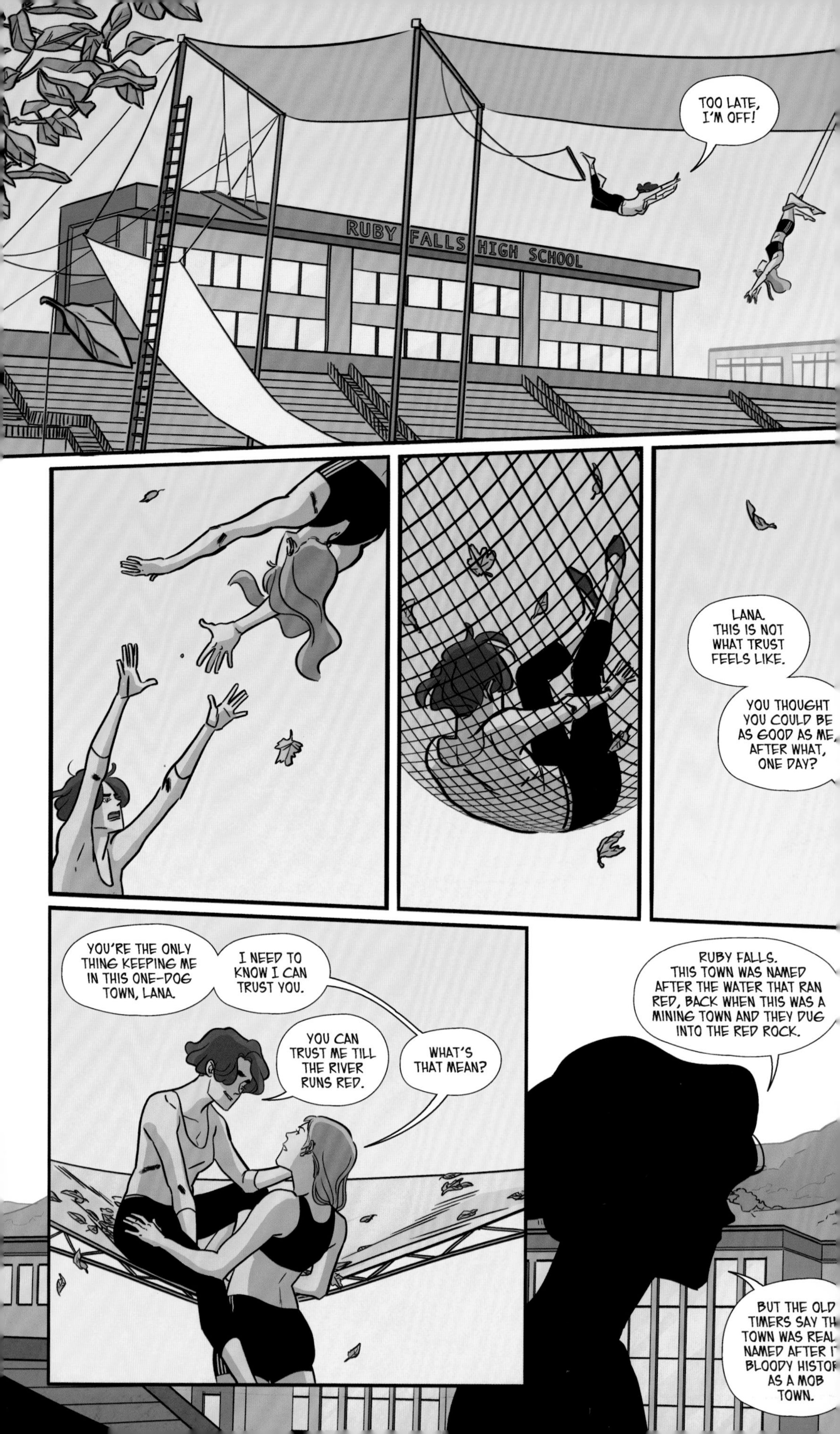
RUBY FALLS HIGH SCHOOL
TOO LATE, I'M OFF!
LANA. THIS IS NOT WHAT TRUST FEELS LIKE.
YOU THOUGHT YOU COULD BE AS GOOD AS ME, AFTER WHAT, ONE DAY?
YOU'RE THE ONLY THING KEEPING ME IN THIS ONE-DOG TOWN, LANA.
I NEED TO KNOW I CAN TRUST YOU.
YOU CAN TRUST ME TILL THE RIVER RUNS RED.
WHAT'S THAT MEAN?
RUBY FALLS. THIS TOWN WAS NAMED AFTER THE WATER THAT RAN RED, BACK WHEN THIS WAS A MINING TOWN AND THEY DUG INTO THE RED ROCK.
BUT THE OLD TIMERS SAY TH TOWN WAS REAL NAMED AFTER I BLOODY HISTOR AS A MOB TOWN.

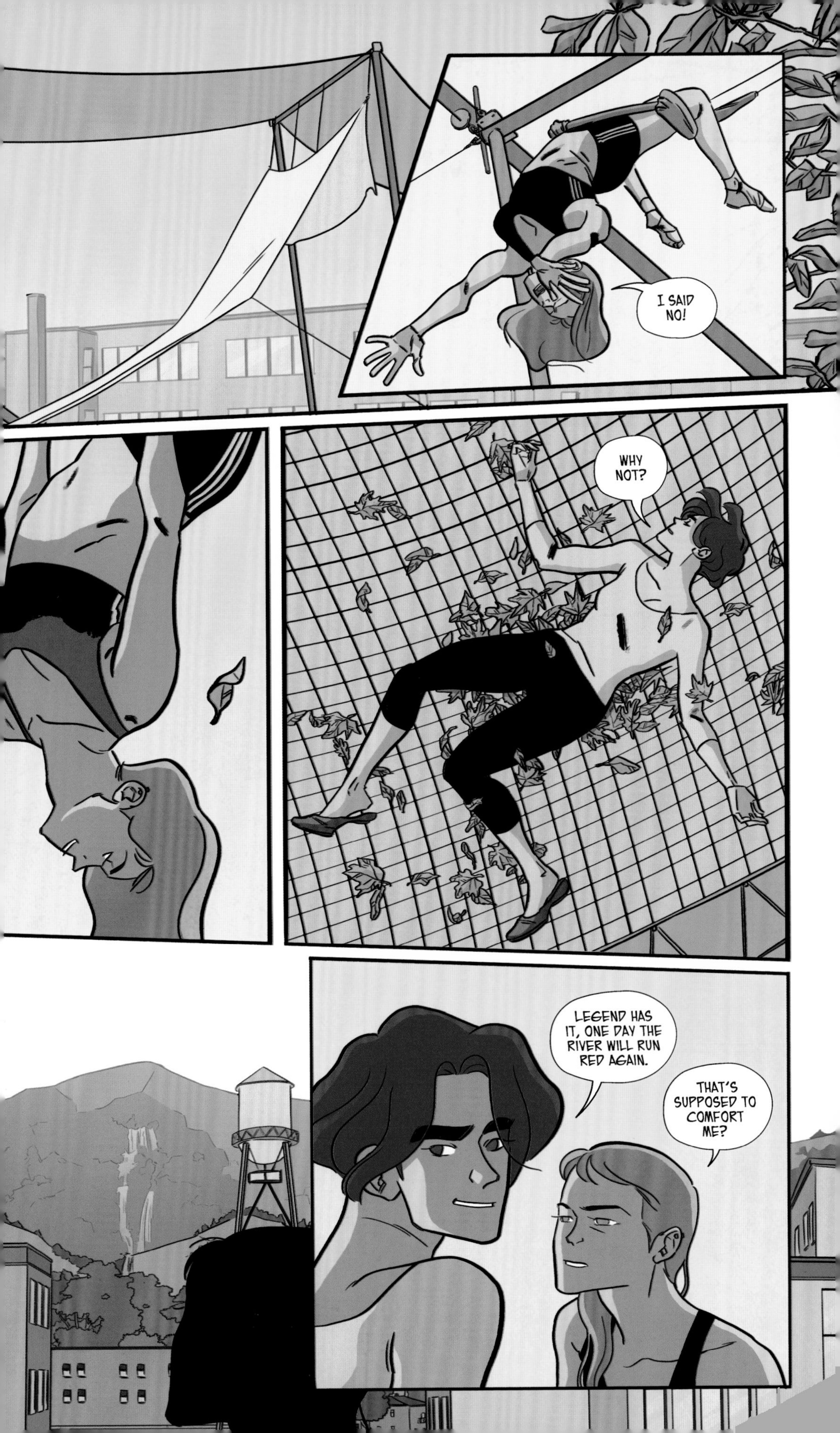
I SAID NO!
WHY NOT?
LEGEND HAS IT, ONE DAY THE RIVER WILL RUN RED AGAIN.
THAT'S SUPPOSED TO COMFORT ME?

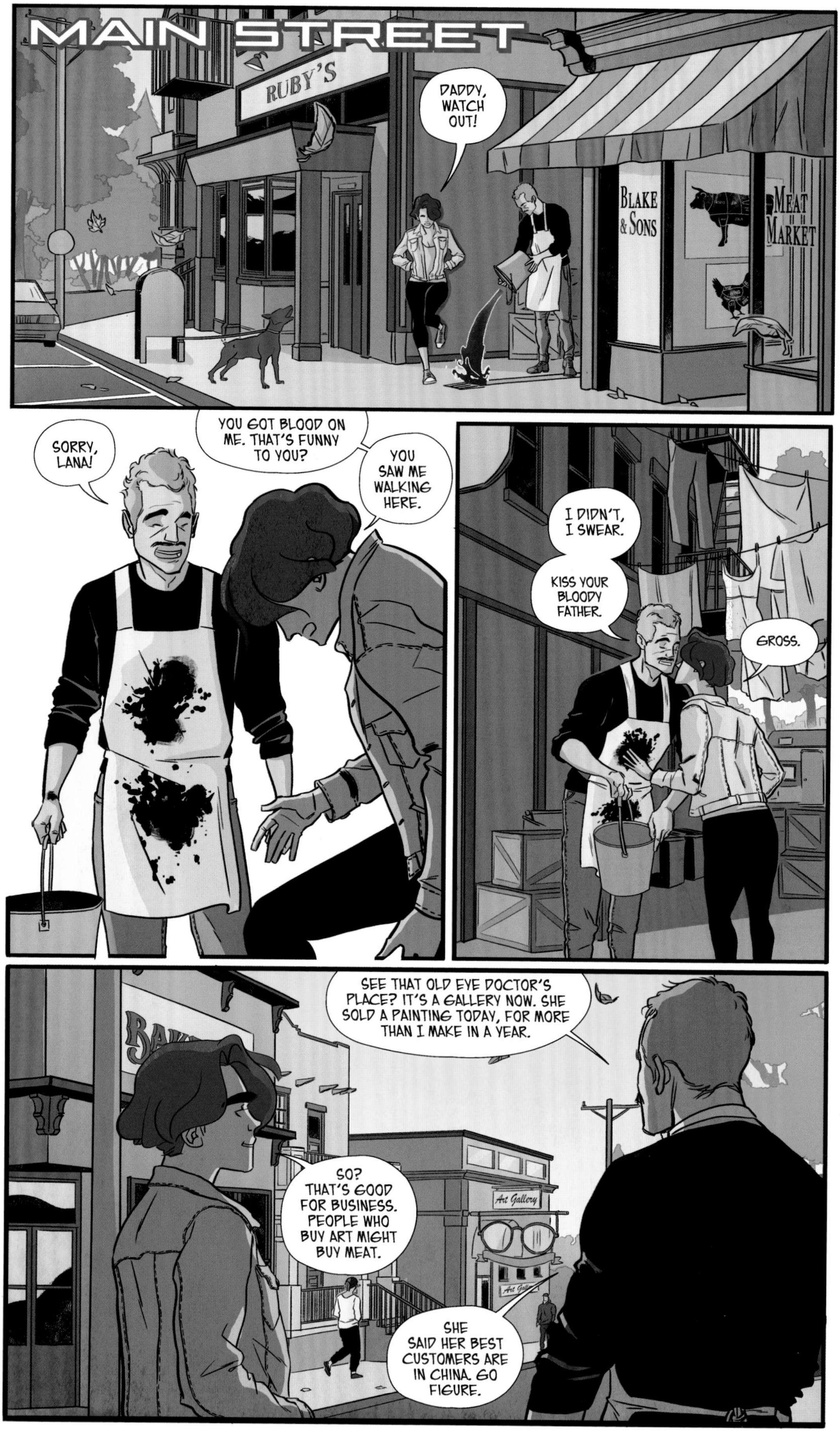
MAIN STREET
RUBY'S
DADDY, WATCH OUT!
BLAKE & SONS
MEAT MARKET
SORRY, LANA!
YOU GOT BLOOD ON ME. THAT'S FUNNY TO YOU?
YOU SAW ME WALKING HERE.
I DIDN'T, I SWEAR.
KISS YOUR BLOODY FATHER.
GROSS.
SEE THAT OLD EYE DOCTOR'S PLACE? IT'S A GALLERY NOW. SHE SOLD A PAINTING TODAY, FOR MORE THAN I MAKE IN A YEAR.
SO? THAT'S GOOD FOR BUSINESS. PEOPLE WHO BUY ART MIGHT BUY MEAT.
Art Gallery
SHE SAID HER BEST CUSTOMERS ARE IN CHINA. GO FIGURE.

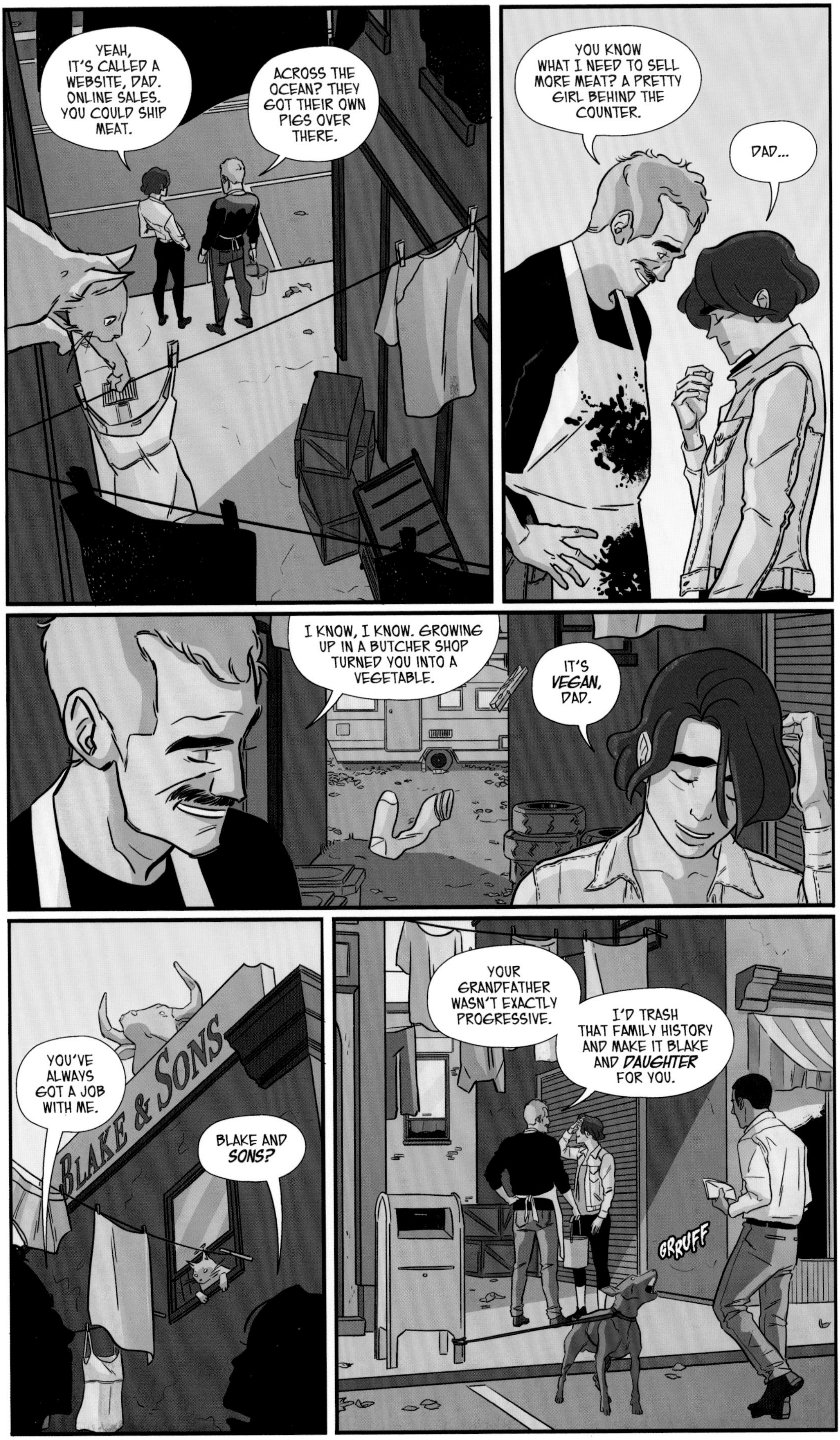
YEAH, IT'S CALLED A WEBSITE, DAD. ONLINE SALES. YOU COULD SHIP MEAT.
ACROSS THE OCEAN? THEY GOT THEIR OWN PIGS OVER THERE.
YOU KNOW WHAT I NEED TO SELL MORE MEAT? A PRETTY GIRL BEHIND THE COUNTER.
DAD...
I KNOW, I KNOW. GROWING UP IN A BUTCHER SHOP TURNED YOU INTO A VEGETABLE.
IT'S *VEGAN,* DAD.
BLAKE & SONS
YOU'VE ALWAYS GOT A JOB WITH ME.
BLAKE AND *SONS?*
YOUR GRANDFATHER WASN'T EXACTLY PROGRESSIVE.
I'D TRASH THAT FAMILY HISTORY AND MAKE IT BLAKE AND *DAUGHTER* FOR YOU.
GRRUFF

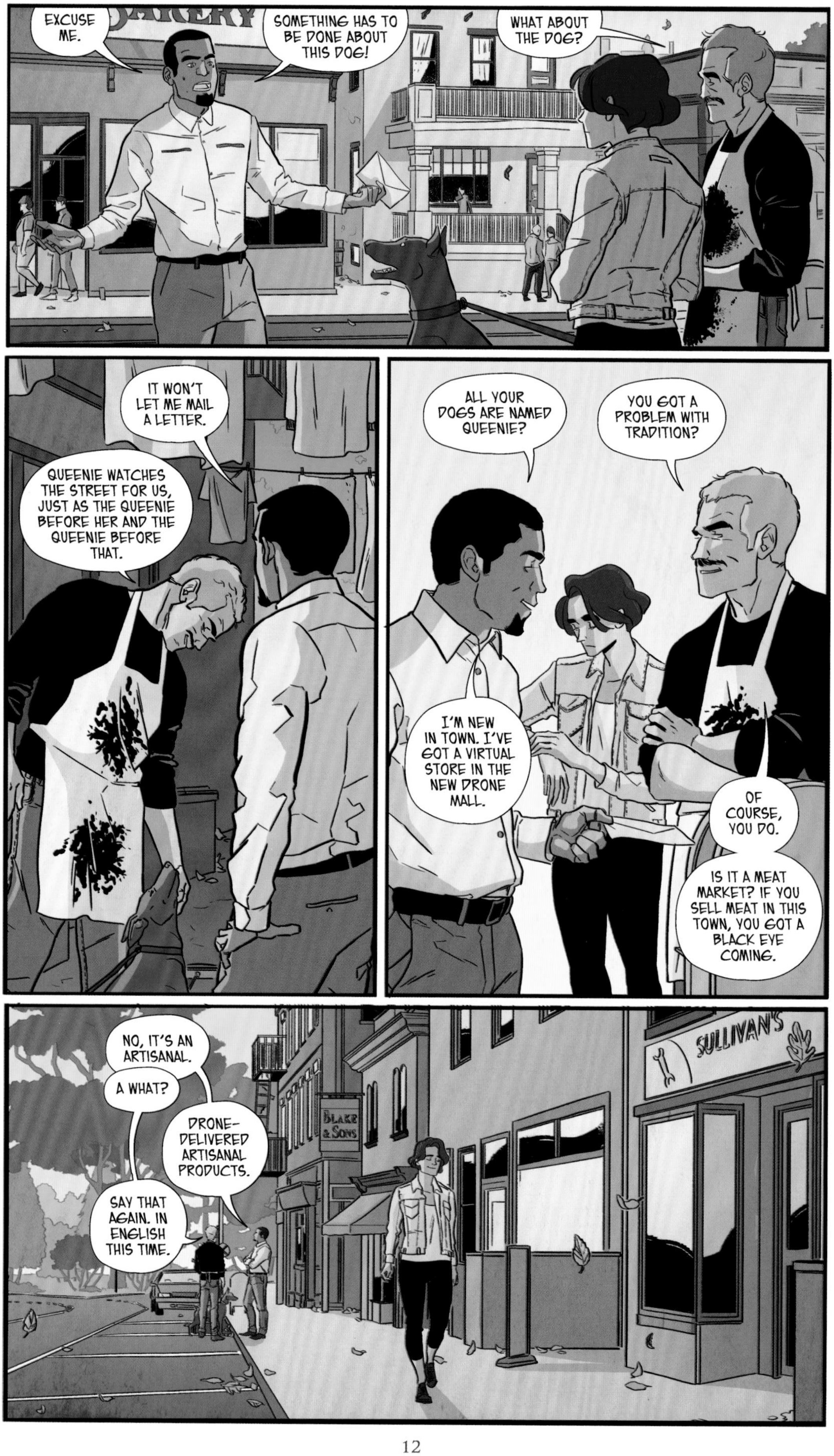

BAKERY
EXCUSE ME.
SOMETHING HAS TO BE DONE ABOUT THIS DOG!
WHAT ABOUT THE DOG?
IT WON'T LET ME MAIL A LETTER.
QUEENIE WATCHES THE STREET FOR US, JUST AS THE QUEENIE BEFORE HER AND THE QUEENIE BEFORE THAT.
ALL YOUR DOGS ARE NAMED QUEENIE?
YOU GOT A PROBLEM WITH TRADITION?
I'M NEW IN TOWN. I'VE GOT A VIRTUAL STORE IN THE NEW DRONE MALL.
OF COURSE, YOU DO.
IS IT A MEAT MARKET? IF YOU SELL MEAT IN THIS TOWN, YOU GOT A BLACK EYE COMING.
NO, IT'S AN ARTISANAL.
A WHAT?
DRONE-DELIVERED ARTISANAL PRODUCTS.
SAY THAT AGAIN. IN ENGLISH THIS TIME.
BLAKE & SONS
SULLIVAN'S

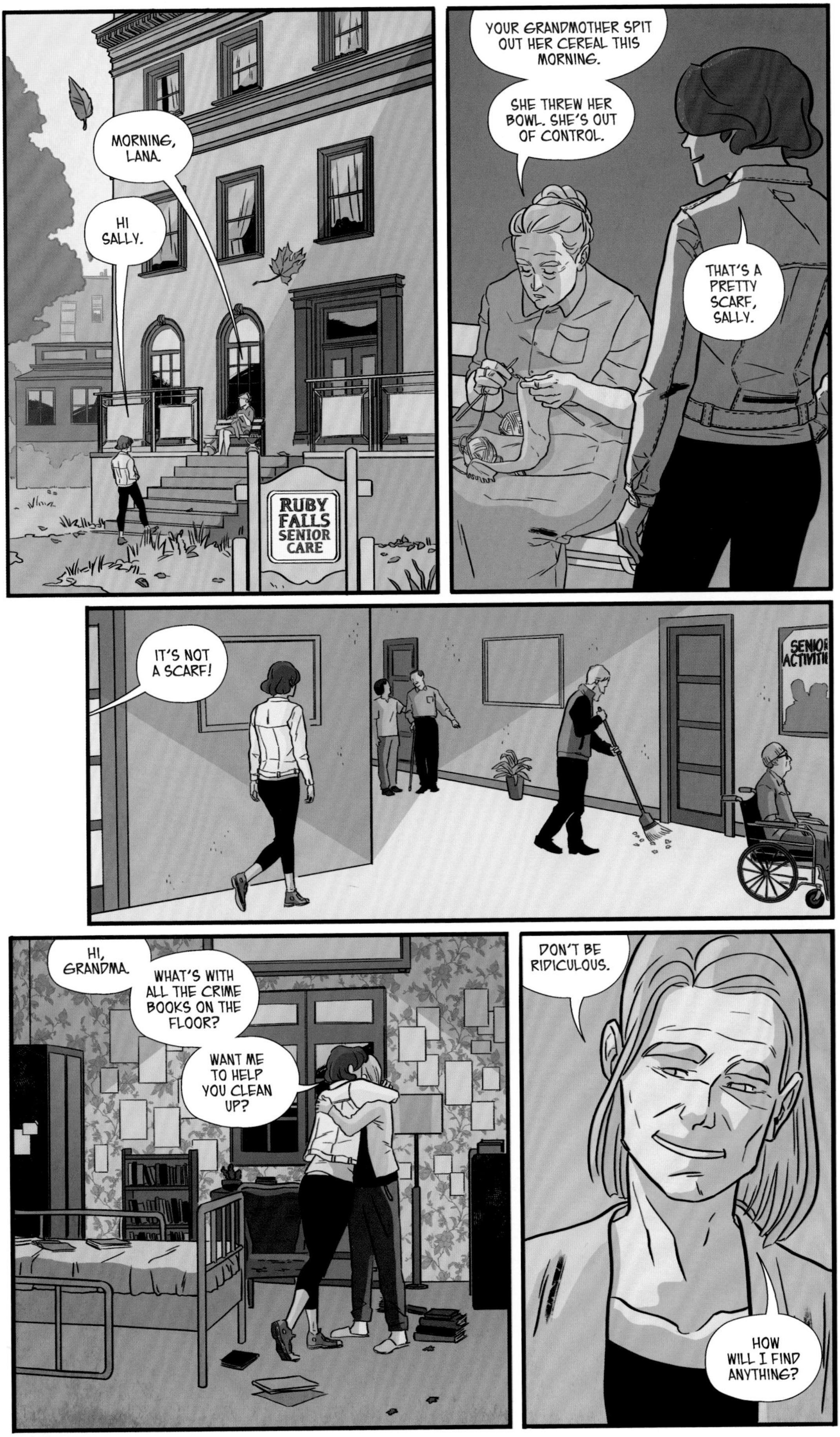
MORNING, LANA.
HI SALLY.
RUBY FALLS SENIOR CARE
YOUR GRANDMOTHER SPIT OUT HER CEREAL THIS MORNING.
SHE THREW HER BOWL. SHE'S OUT OF CONTROL.
THAT'S A PRETTY SCARF, SALLY.
IT'S NOT A SCARF!
HI, GRANDMA.
WHAT'S WITH ALL THE CRIME BOOKS ON THE FLOOR?
WANT ME TO HELP YOU CLEAN UP?
DON'T BE RIDICULOUS.
HOW WILL I FIND ANYTHING?

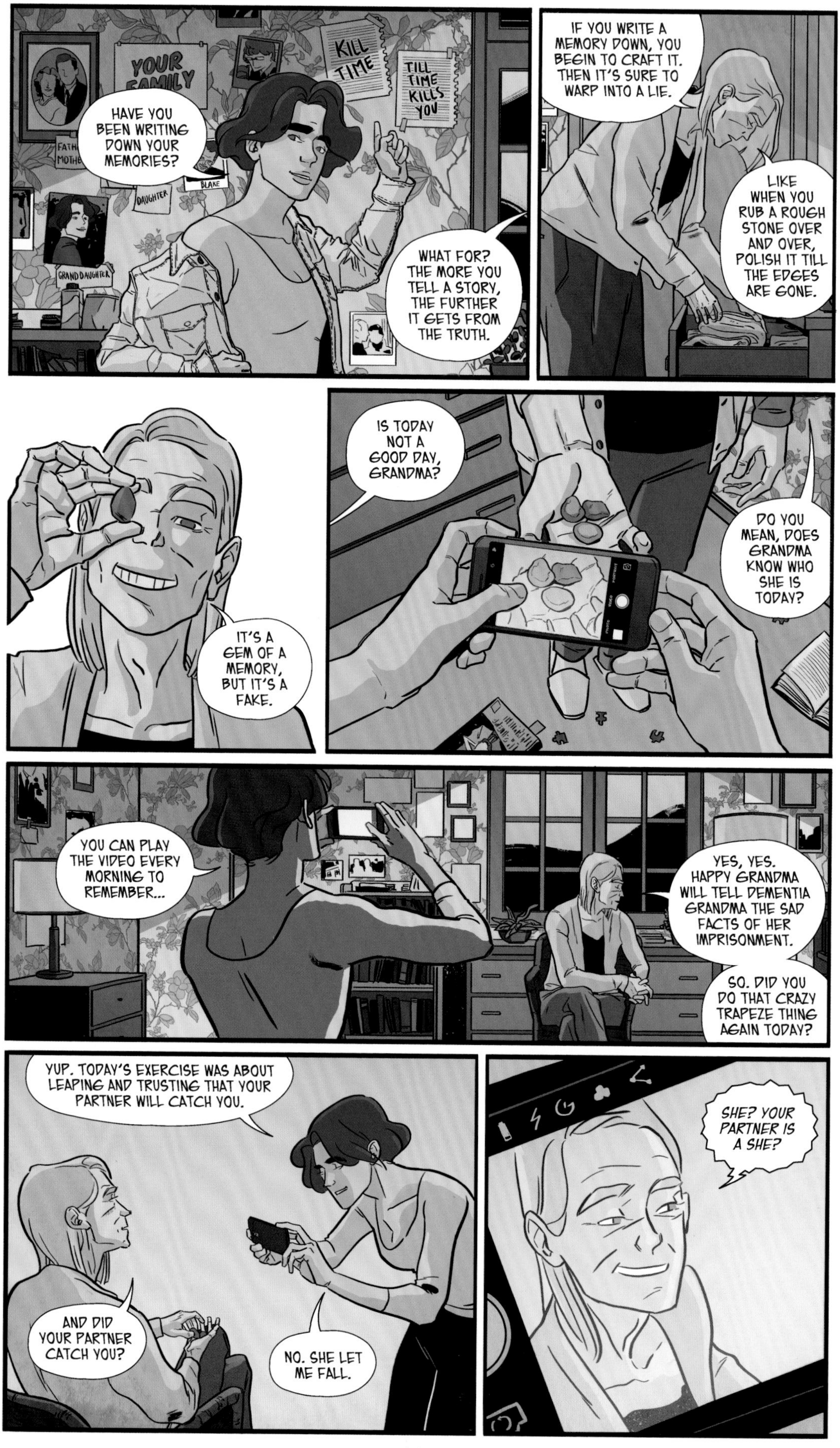
YOUR FAMILY
KILL TIME
TILL TIME KILLS YOU
HAVE YOU BEEN WRITING DOWN YOUR MEMORIES?
BLAKE
DAUGHTER
GRANDDAUGHTER
WHAT FOR? THE MORE YOU TELL A STORY, THE FURTHER IT GETS FROM THE TRUTH.
IF YOU WRITE A MEMORY DOWN, YOU BEGIN TO CRAFT IT. THEN IT'S SURE TO WARP INTO A LIE.
LIKE WHEN YOU RUB A ROUGH STONE OVER AND OVER, POLISH IT TILL THE EDGES ARE GONE.
IT'S A GEM OF A MEMORY, BUT IT'S A FAKE.
IS TODAY NOT A GOOD DAY, GRANDMA?
DO YOU MEAN, DOES GRANDMA KNOW WHO SHE IS TODAY?
YOU CAN PLAY THE VIDEO EVERY MORNING TO REMEMBER...
YES, YES. HAPPY GRANDMA WILL TELL DEMENTIA GRANDMA THE SAD FACTS OF HER IMPRISONMENT.
SO. DID YOU DO THAT CRAZY TRAPEZE THING AGAIN TODAY?
YUP. TODAY'S EXERCISE WAS ABOUT LEAPING AND TRUSTING THAT YOUR PARTNER WILL CATCH YOU.
AND DID YOUR PARTNER CATCH YOU?
NO. SHE LET ME FALL.
SHE? YOUR PARTNER IS A SHE?

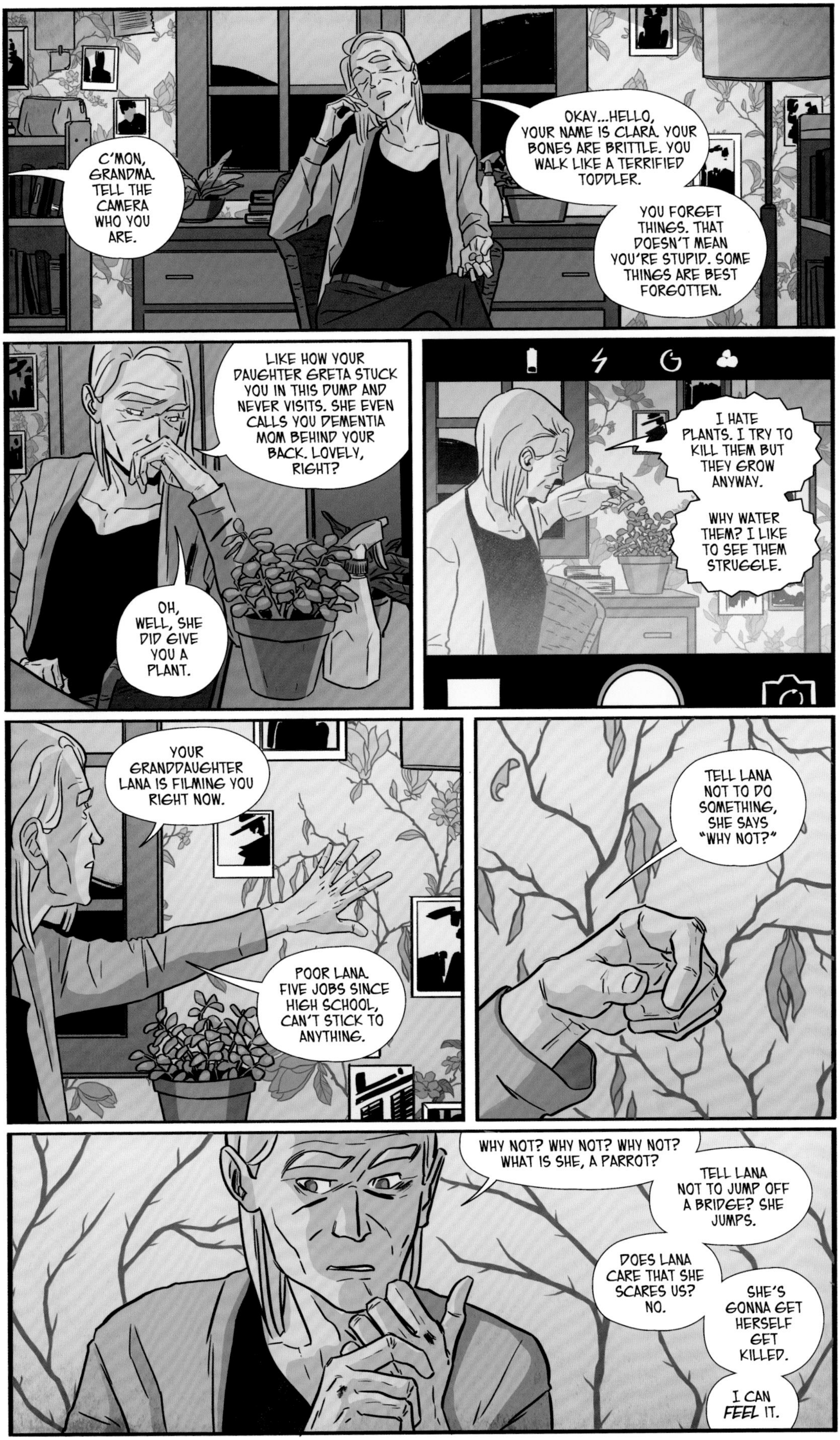
C'MON, GRANDMA. TELL THE CAMERA WHO YOU ARE.
OKAY...HELLO, YOUR NAME IS CLARA. YOUR BONES ARE BRITTLE. YOU WALK LIKE A TERRIFIED TODDLER.
YOU FORGET THINGS. THAT DOESN'T MEAN YOU'RE STUPID. SOME THINGS ARE BEST FORGOTTEN.
LIKE HOW YOUR DAUGHTER GRETA STUCK YOU IN THIS DUMP AND NEVER VISITS. SHE EVEN CALLS YOU DEMENTIA MOM BEHIND YOUR BACK. LOVELY, RIGHT?
OH, WELL, SHE DID GIVE YOU A PLANT.
I HATE PLANTS. I TRY TO KILL THEM BUT THEY GROW ANYWAY.
WHY WATER THEM? I LIKE TO SEE THEM STRUGGLE.
YOUR GRANDDAUGHTER LANA IS FILMING YOU RIGHT NOW.
POOR LANA. FIVE JOBS SINCE HIGH SCHOOL, CAN'T STICK TO ANYTHING.
TELL LANA NOT TO DO SOMETHING, SHE SAYS "WHY NOT?"
WHY NOT? WHY NOT? WHY NOT? WHAT IS SHE, A PARROT?
TELL LANA NOT TO JUMP OFF A BRIDGE? SHE JUMPS.
DOES LANA CARE THAT SHE SCARES US? NO.
SHE'S GONNA GET HERSELF GET KILLED.
I CAN *FEEL* IT.

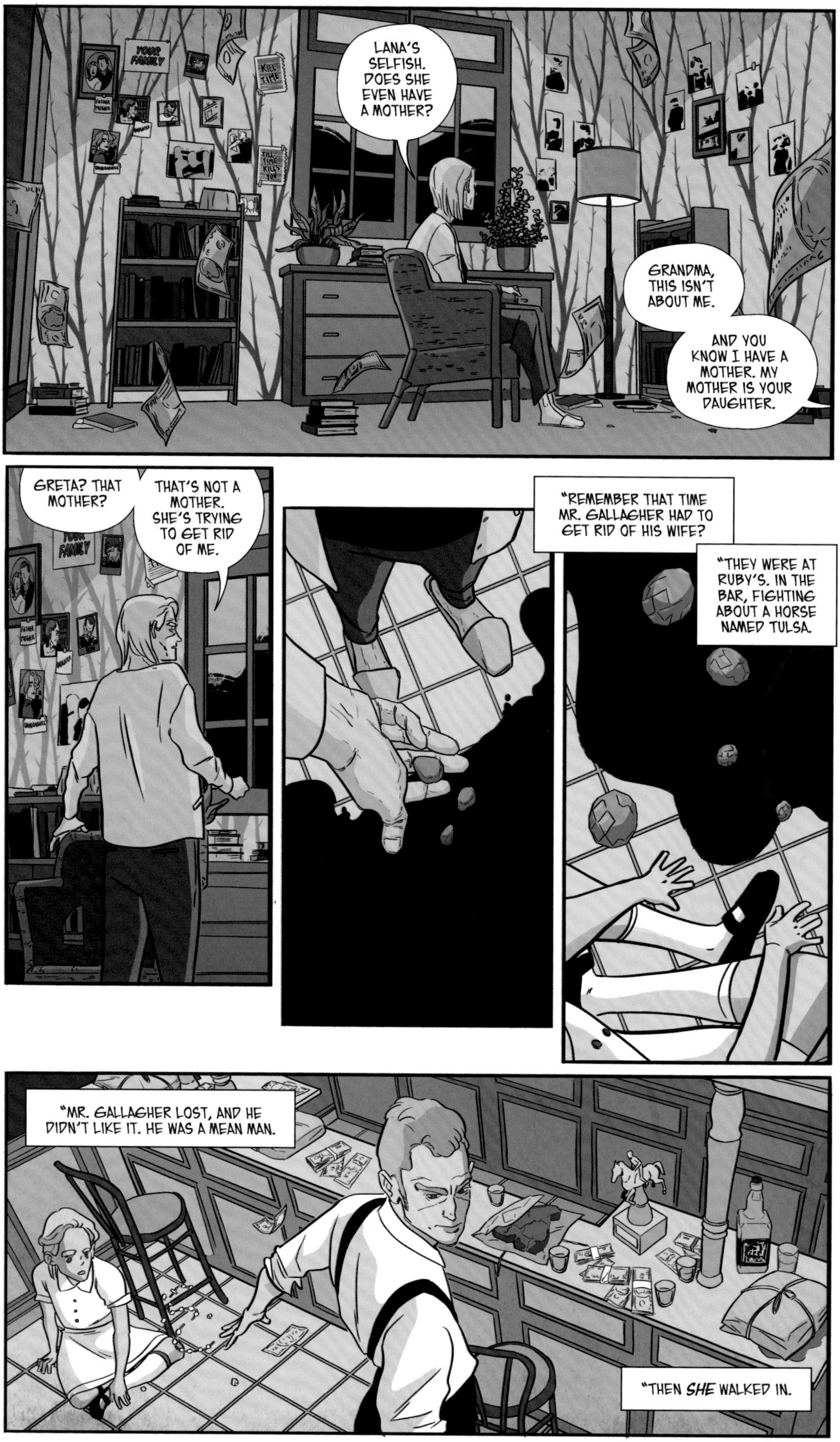
LANA'S SELFISH. DOES SHE EVEN HAVE A MOTHER?
GRANDMA, THIS ISN'T ABOUT ME.
AND YOU KNOW I HAVE A MOTHER. MY MOTHER IS YOUR DAUGHTER.
GRETA? THAT MOTHER?
THAT'S NOT A MOTHER. SHE'S TRYING TO GET RID OF ME.
"REMEMBER THAT TIME MR. GALLAGHER HAD TO GET RID OF HIS WIFE?
"THEY WERE AT RUBY'S. IN THE BAR, FIGHTING ABOUT A HORSE NAMED TULSA.
"MR. GALLAGHER LOST, AND HE DIDN'T LIKE IT. HE WAS A MEAN MAN.
"THEN *SHE* WALKED IN.

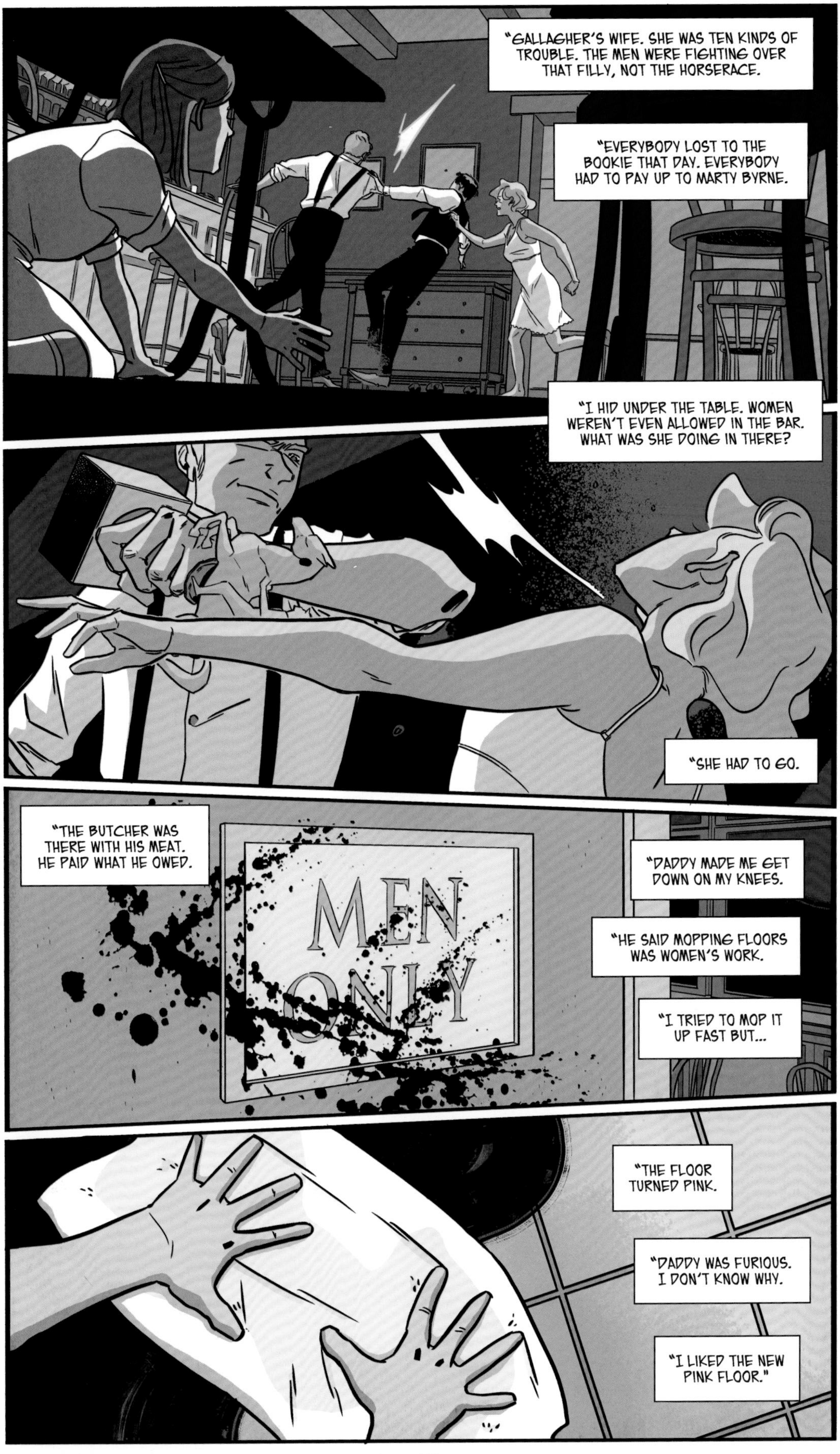
"GALLAGHER'S WIFE. SHE WAS TEN KINDS OF TROUBLE. THE MEN WERE FIGHTING OVER THAT FILLY, NOT THE HORSERACE.
"EVERYBODY LOST TO THE BOOKIE THAT DAY. EVERYBODY HAD TO PAY UP TO MARTY BYRNE.
"I HID UNDER THE TABLE. WOMEN WEREN'T EVEN ALLOWED IN THE BAR. WHAT WAS SHE DOING IN THERE?
"SHE HAD TO GO.
"THE BUTCHER WAS THERE WITH HIS MEAT. HE PAID WHAT HE OWED.
MEN ONLY
"DADDY MADE ME GET DOWN ON MY KNEES.
"HE SAID MOPPING FLOORS WAS WOMEN'S WORK.
"I TRIED TO MOP IT UP FAST BUT...
"THE FLOOR TURNED PINK.
"DADDY WAS FURIOUS. I DON'T KNOW WHY.
"I LIKED THE NEW PINK FLOOR."

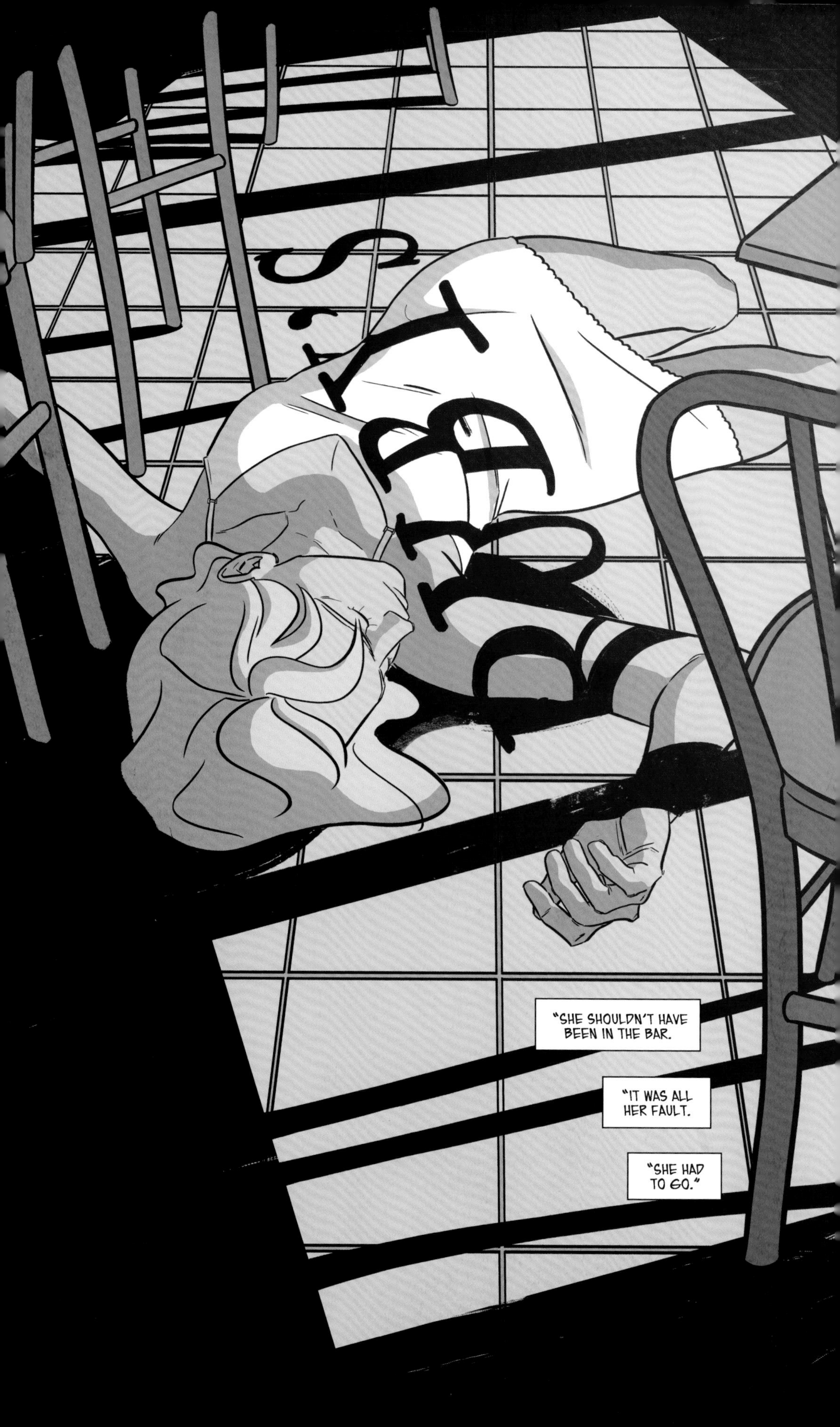
"SHE SHOULDN'T HAVE BEEN IN THE BAR.
"IT WAS ALL HER FAULT.
"SHE HAD TO GO."

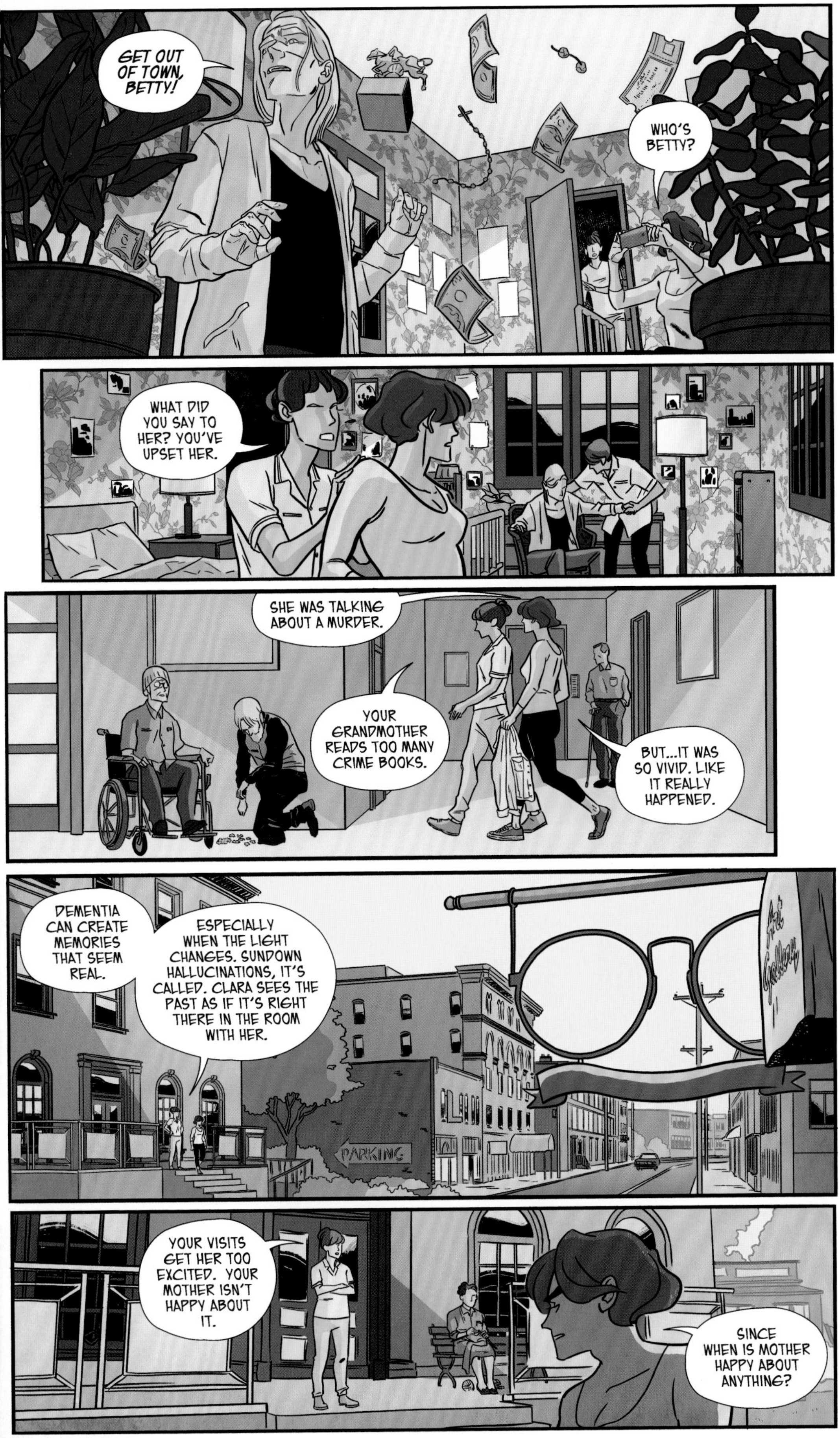
GET OUT OF TOWN, BETTY!
WHO'S BETTY?
WHAT DID YOU SAY TO HER? YOU'VE UPSET HER.
SHE WAS TALKING ABOUT A MURDER.
YOUR GRANDMOTHER READS TOO MANY CRIME BOOKS.
BUT...IT WAS SO VIVID. LIKE IT REALLY HAPPENED.
DEMENTIA CAN CREATE MEMORIES THAT SEEM REAL.
ESPECIALLY WHEN THE LIGHT CHANGES. SUNDOWN HALLUCINATIONS, IT'S CALLED. CLARA SEES THE PAST AS IF IT'S RIGHT THERE IN THE ROOM WITH HER.
PARKING
YOUR VISITS GET HER TOO EXCITED. YOUR MOTHER ISN'T HAPPY ABOUT IT.
SINCE WHEN IS MOTHER HAPPY ABOUT ANYTHING?

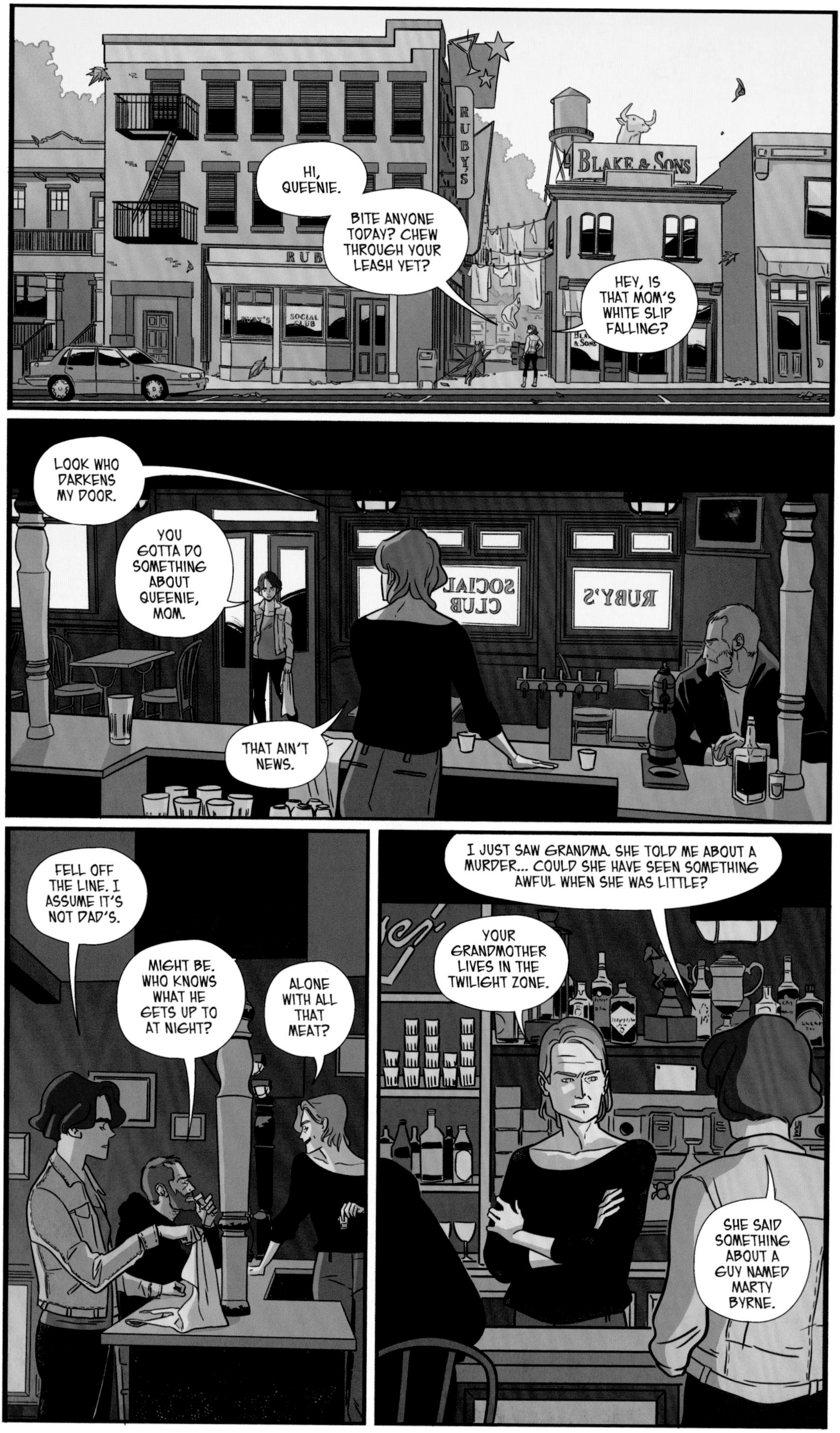

BLAKE & SONS
HI, QUEENIE.
BITE ANYONE TODAY? CHEW THROUGH YOUR LEASH YET?
HEY, IS THAT MOM'S WHITE SLIP FALLING?
LOOK WHO DARKENS MY DOOR.
YOU GOTTA DO SOMETHING ABOUT QUEENIE, MOM.
THAT AIN'T NEWS.
FELL OFF THE LINE. I ASSUME IT'S NOT DAD'S.
MIGHT BE. WHO KNOWS WHAT HE GETS UP TO AT NIGHT?
ALONE WITH ALL THAT MEAT?
I JUST SAW GRANDMA. SHE TOLD ME ABOUT A MURDER... COULD SHE HAVE SEEN SOMETHING AWFUL WHEN SHE WAS LITTLE?
YOUR GRANDMOTHER LIVES IN THE TWILIGHT ZONE.
SHE SAID SOMETHING ABOUT A GUY NAMED MARTY BYRNE.

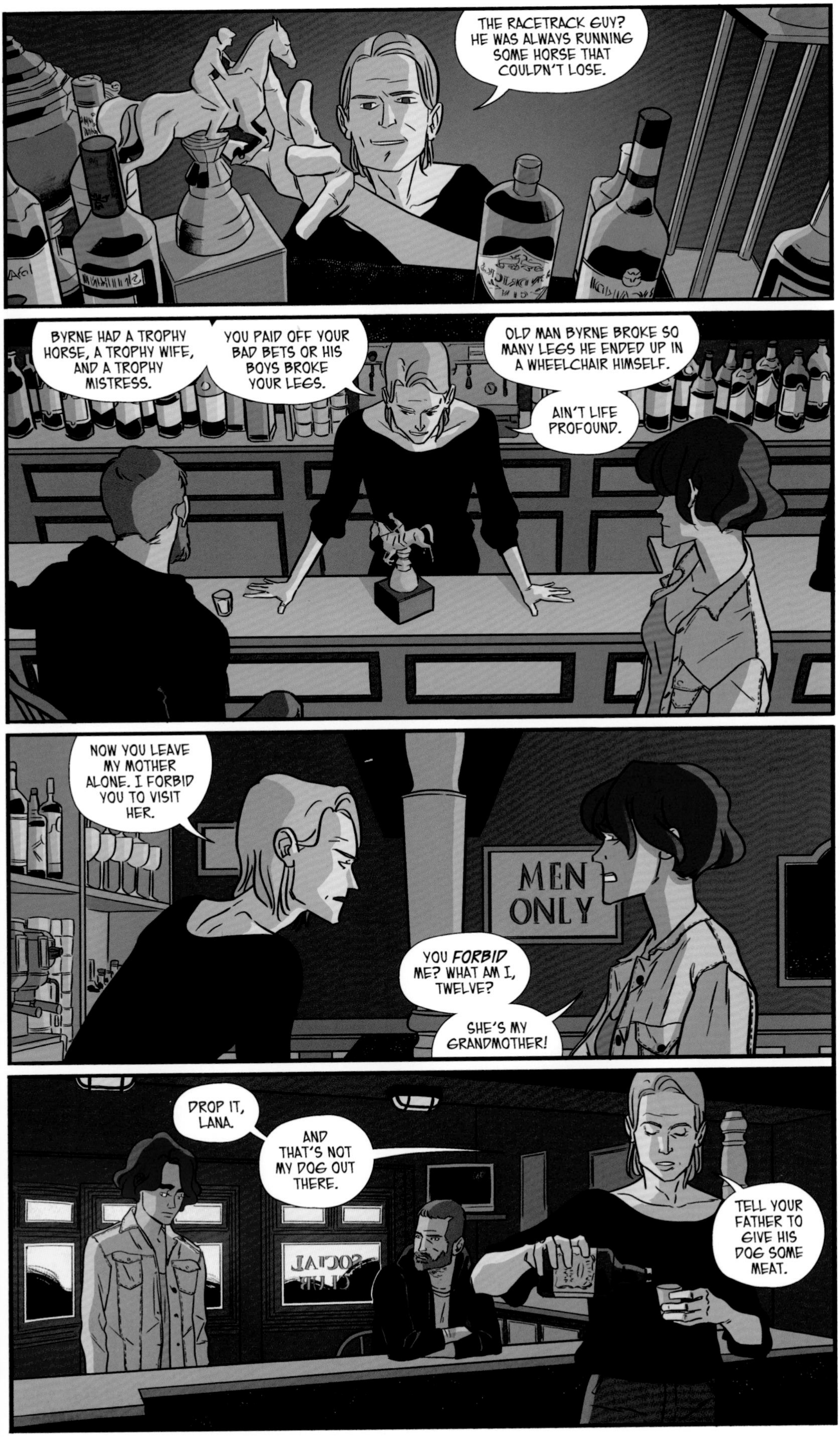
THE RACETRACK GUY? HE WAS ALWAYS RUNNING SOME HORSE THAT COULDN'T LOSE.
BYRNE HAD A TROPHY HORSE, A TROPHY WIFE, AND A TROPHY MISTRESS.
YOU PAID OFF YOUR BAD BETS OR HIS BOYS BROKE YOUR LEGS.
OLD MAN BYRNE BROKE SO MANY LEGS HE ENDED UP IN A WHEELCHAIR HIMSELF.
AIN'T LIFE PROFOUND.
NOW YOU LEAVE MY MOTHER ALONE. I FORBID YOU TO VISIT HER.
MEN ONLY
YOU *FORBID* ME? WHAT AM I, TWELVE?
SHE'S MY GRANDMOTHER!
DROP IT, LANA.
AND THAT'S NOT MY DOG OUT THERE.
TELL YOUR FATHER TO GIVE HIS DOG SOME MEAT.

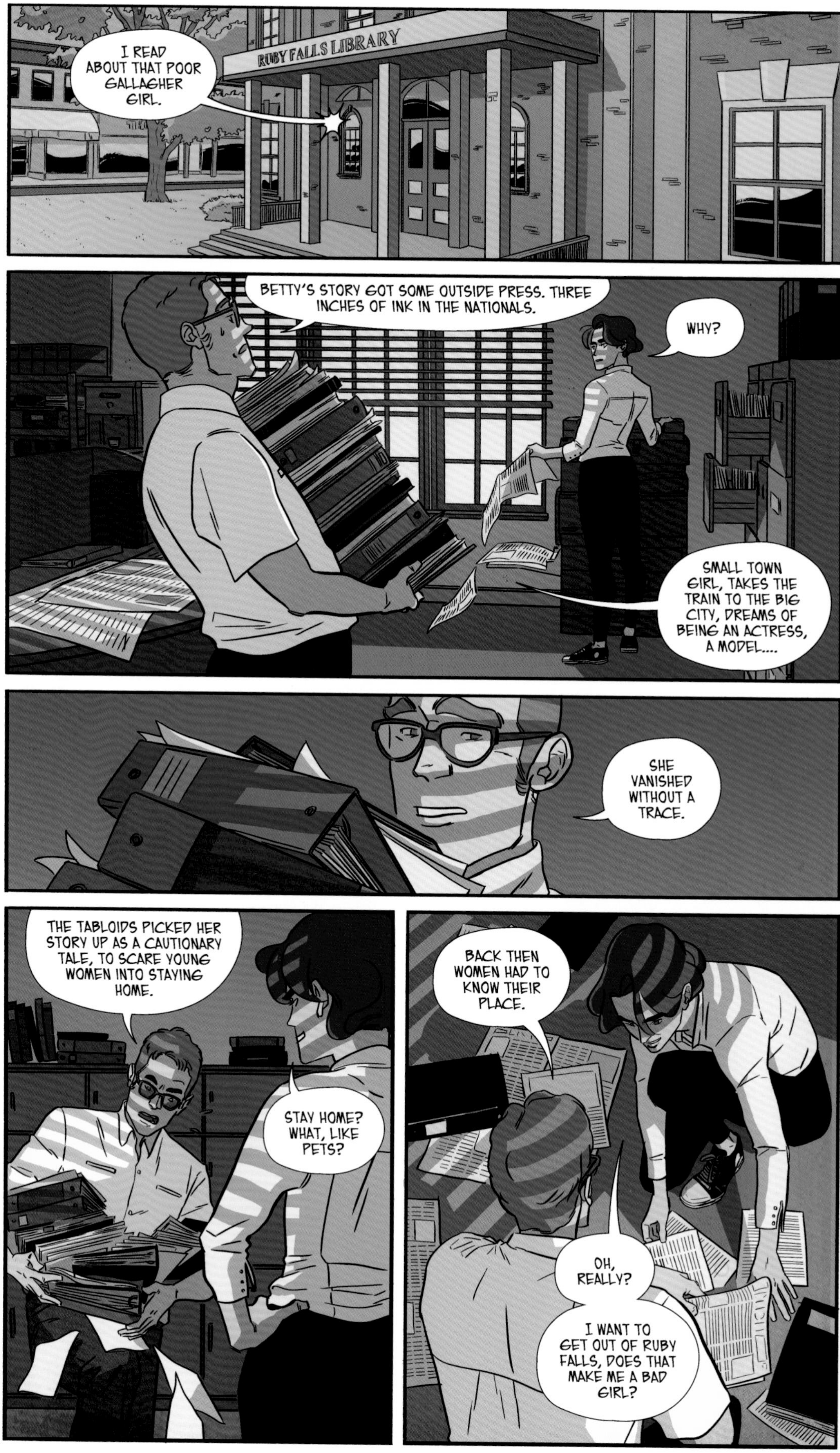
RUBY FALLS LIBRARY
I READ ABOUT THAT POOR GALLAGHER GIRL.
BETTY'S STORY GOT SOME OUTSIDE PRESS. THREE INCHES OF INK IN THE NATIONALS.
WHY?
SMALL TOWN GIRL, TAKES THE TRAIN TO THE BIG CITY, DREAMS OF BEING AN ACTRESS, A MODEL....
SHE VANISHED WITHOUT A TRACE.
THE TABLOIDS PICKED HER STORY UP AS A CAUTIONARY TALE, TO SCARE YOUNG WOMEN INTO STAYING HOME.
STAY HOME? WHAT, LIKE PETS?
BACK THEN WOMEN HAD TO KNOW THEIR PLACE.
OH, REALLY?
I WANT TO GET OUT OF RUBY FALLS, DOES THAT MAKE ME A BAD GIRL?

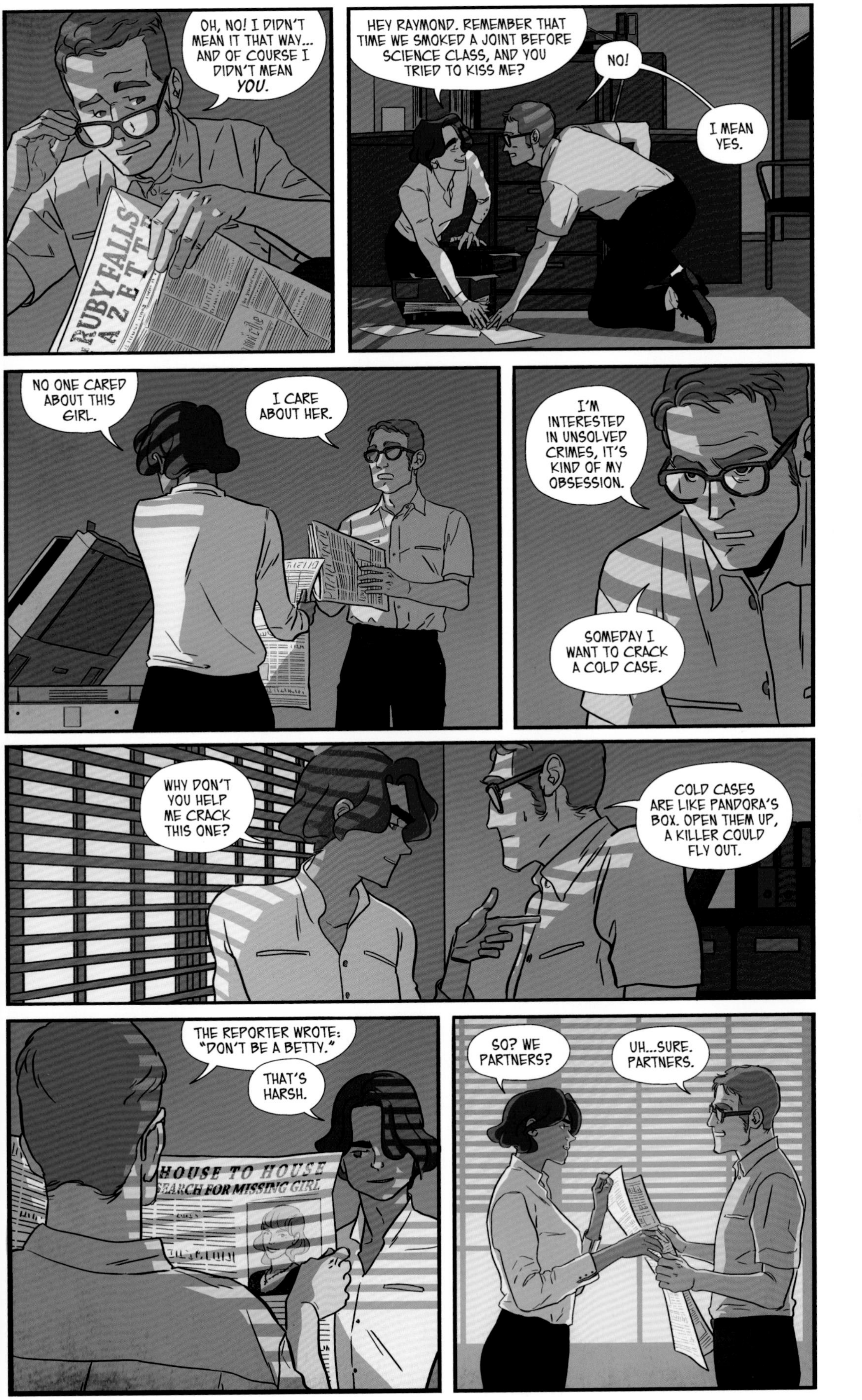
OH, NO! I DIDN'T MEAN IT THAT WAY... AND OF COURSE I DIDN'T MEAN *YOU*.
RUBY FALLS GAZETTE
HEY RAYMOND. REMEMBER THAT TIME WE SMOKED A JOINT BEFORE SCIENCE CLASS, AND YOU TRIED TO KISS ME?
NO!
I MEAN YES.
NO ONE CARED ABOUT THIS GIRL.
I CARE ABOUT HER.
I'M INTERESTED IN UNSOLVED CRIMES, IT'S KIND OF MY OBSESSION.
SOMEDAY I WANT TO CRACK A COLD CASE.
WHY DON'T YOU HELP ME CRACK THIS ONE?
COLD CASES ARE LIKE PANDORA'S BOX. OPEN THEM UP, A KILLER COULD FLY OUT.
THE REPORTER WROTE: "DON'T BE A BETTY."
THAT'S HARSH.
HOUSE TO HOUSE SEARCH FOR MISSING GIRL
SO? WE PARTNERS?
UH...SURE. PARTNERS.

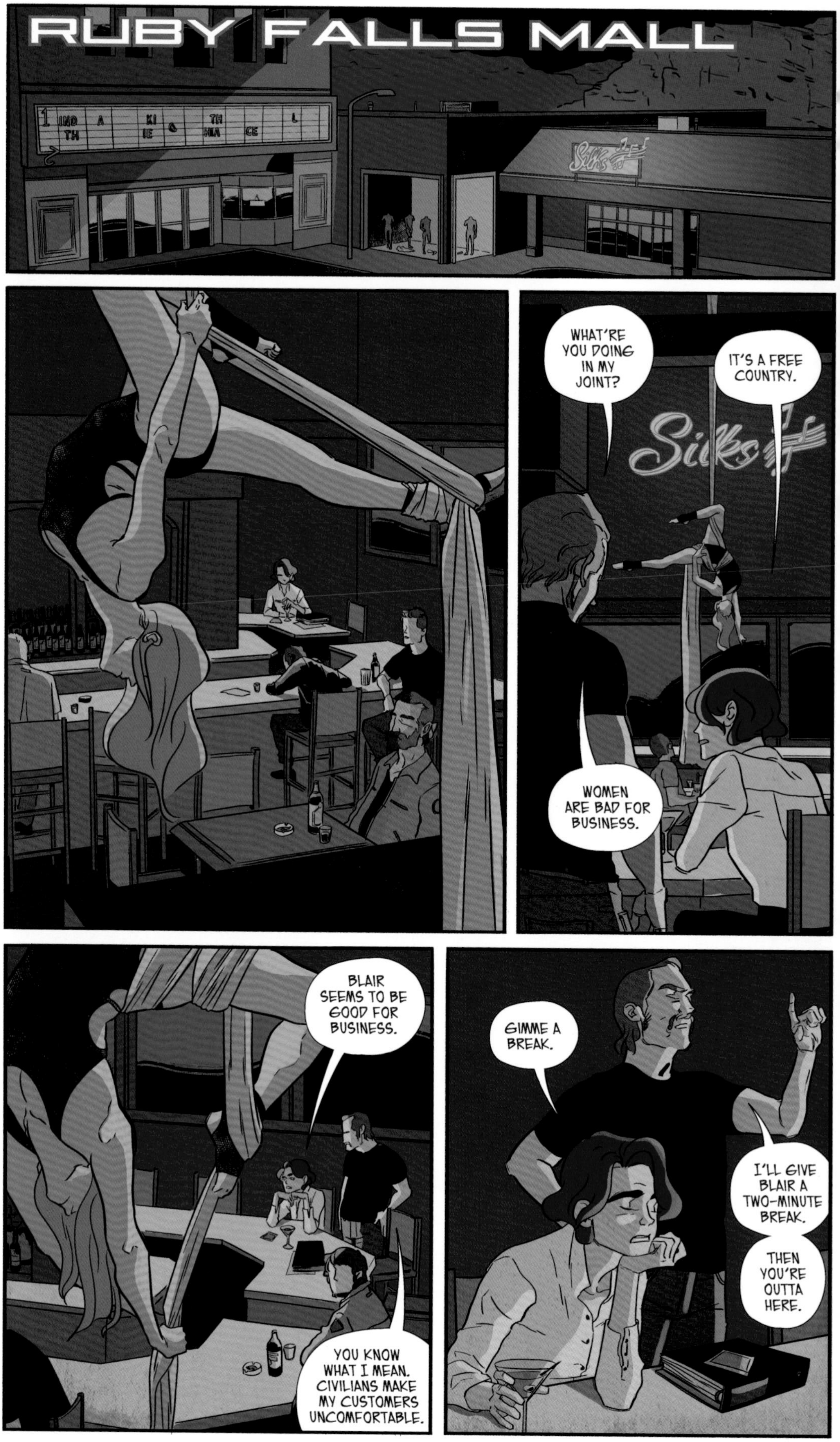
RUBY FALLS MALL
Silks
WHAT'RE YOU DOING IN MY JOINT?
IT'S A FREE COUNTRY.
WOMEN ARE BAD FOR BUSINESS.
BLAIR SEEMS TO BE GOOD FOR BUSINESS.
YOU KNOW WHAT I MEAN. CIVILIANS MAKE MY CUSTOMERS UNCOMFORTABLE.
GIMME A BREAK.
I'LL GIVE BLAIR A TWO-MINUTE BREAK.
THEN YOU'RE OUTTA HERE.

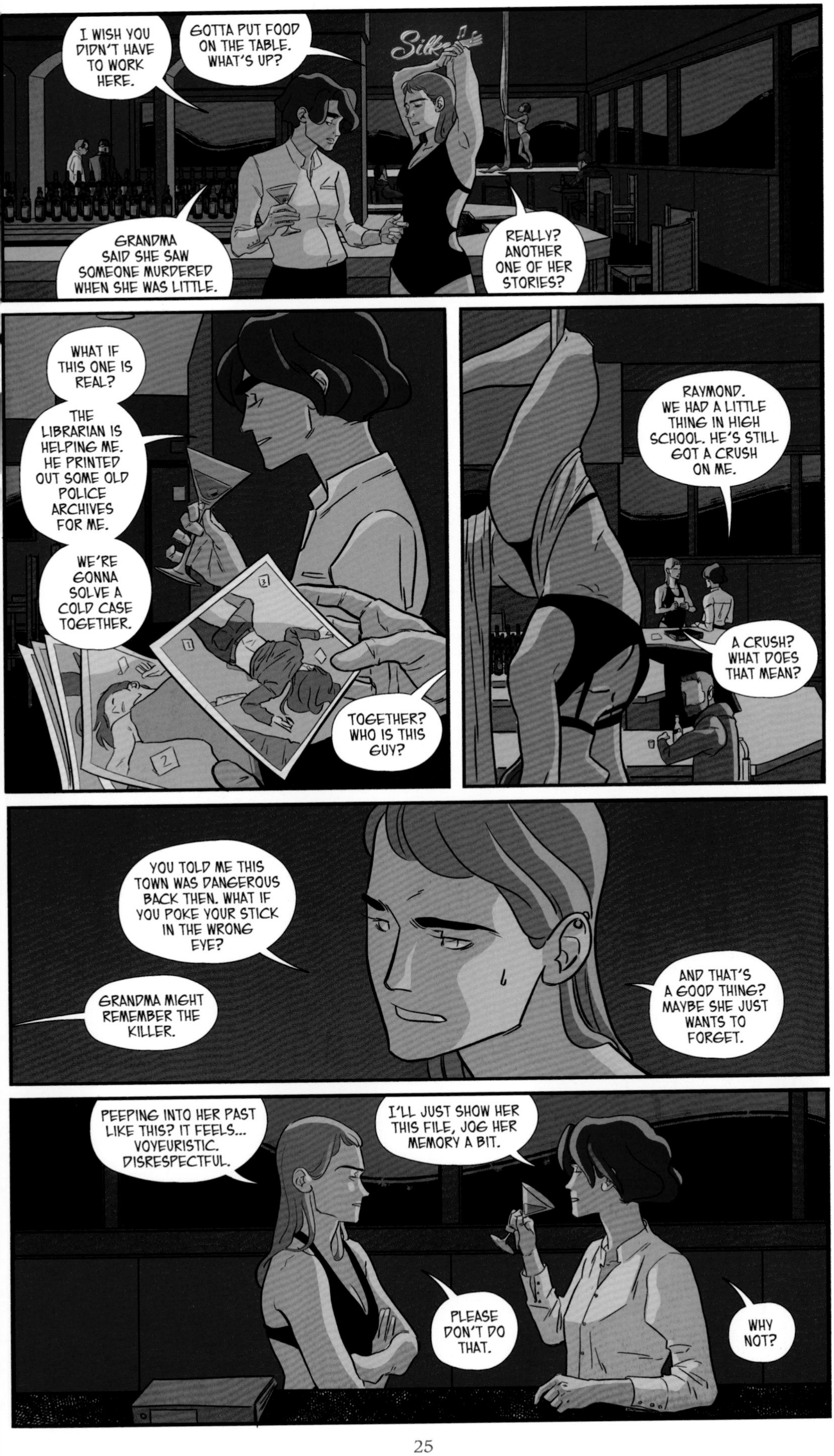
I WISH YOU DIDN'T HAVE TO WORK HERE.
GOTTA PUT FOOD ON THE TABLE. WHAT'S UP?
Silk
GRANDMA SAID SHE SAW SOMEONE MURDERED WHEN SHE WAS LITTLE.
REALLY? ANOTHER ONE OF HER STORIES?
WHAT IF THIS ONE IS REAL?
THE LIBRARIAN IS HELPING ME. HE PRINTED OUT SOME OLD POLICE ARCHIVES FOR ME.
WE'RE GONNA SOLVE A COLD CASE TOGETHER.
TOGETHER? WHO IS THIS GUY?
RAYMOND. WE HAD A LITTLE THING IN HIGH SCHOOL. HE'S STILL GOT A CRUSH ON ME.
A CRUSH? WHAT DOES THAT MEAN?
YOU TOLD ME THIS TOWN WAS DANGEROUS BACK THEN. WHAT IF YOU POKE YOUR STICK IN THE WRONG EYE?
GRANDMA MIGHT REMEMBER THE KILLER.
AND THAT'S A GOOD THING? MAYBE SHE JUST WANTS TO FORGET.
PEEPING INTO HER PAST LIKE THIS? IT FEELS... VOYEURISTIC. DISRESPECTFUL.
I'LL JUST SHOW HER THIS FILE, JOG HER MEMORY A BIT.
PLEASE DON'T DO THAT.
WHY NOT?

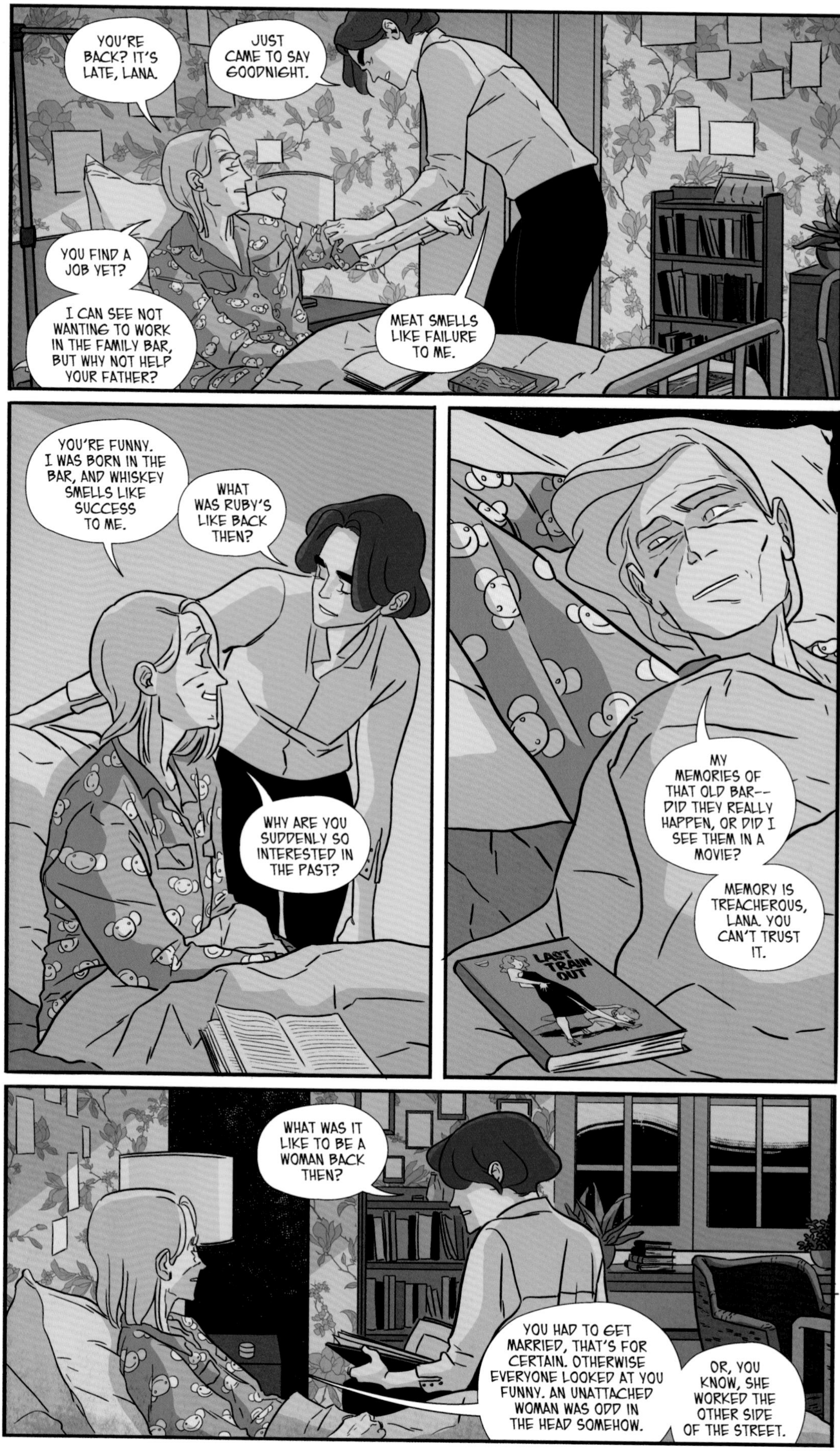
YOU'RE BACK? IT'S LATE, LANA.
JUST CAME TO SAY GOODNIGHT.
YOU FIND A JOB YET?
I CAN SEE NOT WANTING TO WORK IN THE FAMILY BAR, BUT WHY NOT HELP YOUR FATHER?
MEAT SMELLS LIKE FAILURE TO ME.
YOU'RE FUNNY. I WAS BORN IN THE BAR, AND WHISKEY SMELLS LIKE SUCCESS TO ME.
WHAT WAS RUBY'S LIKE BACK THEN?
WHY ARE YOU SUDDENLY SO INTERESTED IN THE PAST?
MY MEMORIES OF THAT OLD BAR--DID THEY REALLY HAPPEN, OR DID I SEE THEM IN A MOVIE?
MEMORY IS TREACHEROUS, LANA. YOU CAN'T TRUST IT.
LAST TRAIN OUT
WHAT WAS IT LIKE TO BE A WOMAN BACK THEN?
YOU HAD TO GET MARRIED, THAT'S FOR CERTAIN. OTHERWISE EVERYONE LOOKED AT YOU FUNNY. AN UNATTACHED WOMAN WAS ODD IN THE HEAD SOMEHOW.
OR, YOU KNOW, SHE WORKED THE OTHER SIDE OF THE STREET.

YOU TOLD ME ABOUT A GUY, MR. GALLAGHER.

YOU SAID HE HAD TO GET RID OF HIS WIFE.

HOUSE TO HOUSE SEARCH FOR MISSING GIRL

IS THIS HER?

GET THIS AWAY FROM ME! I DON'T WANT TO LOOK AT IT!

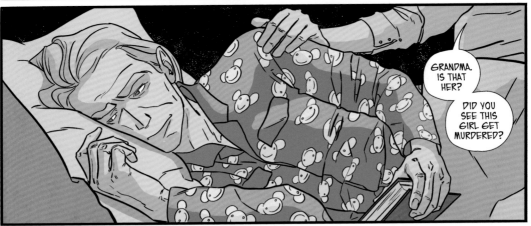

GRANDMA. IS THAT HER?

DID YOU SEE THIS GIRL GET MURDERED?

THAT STORY I TOLD YOU? IT'S FICTION. IT'S FROM A CRAPPY OLD CRIME NOVEL.

STUFF SETTLES TO THE BOTTOM FOR A REASON. *QUIT STIRRING THE POT, BETTY!*

I'M NOT BETTY. WHY DID YOU CALL ME BETTY?

YOU WERE ALWAYS TOO WILD. MAYBE YOUR MOTHER IS RIGHT ABOUT YOU!

DON'T SAY THAT!

LAST TRAIN OUT

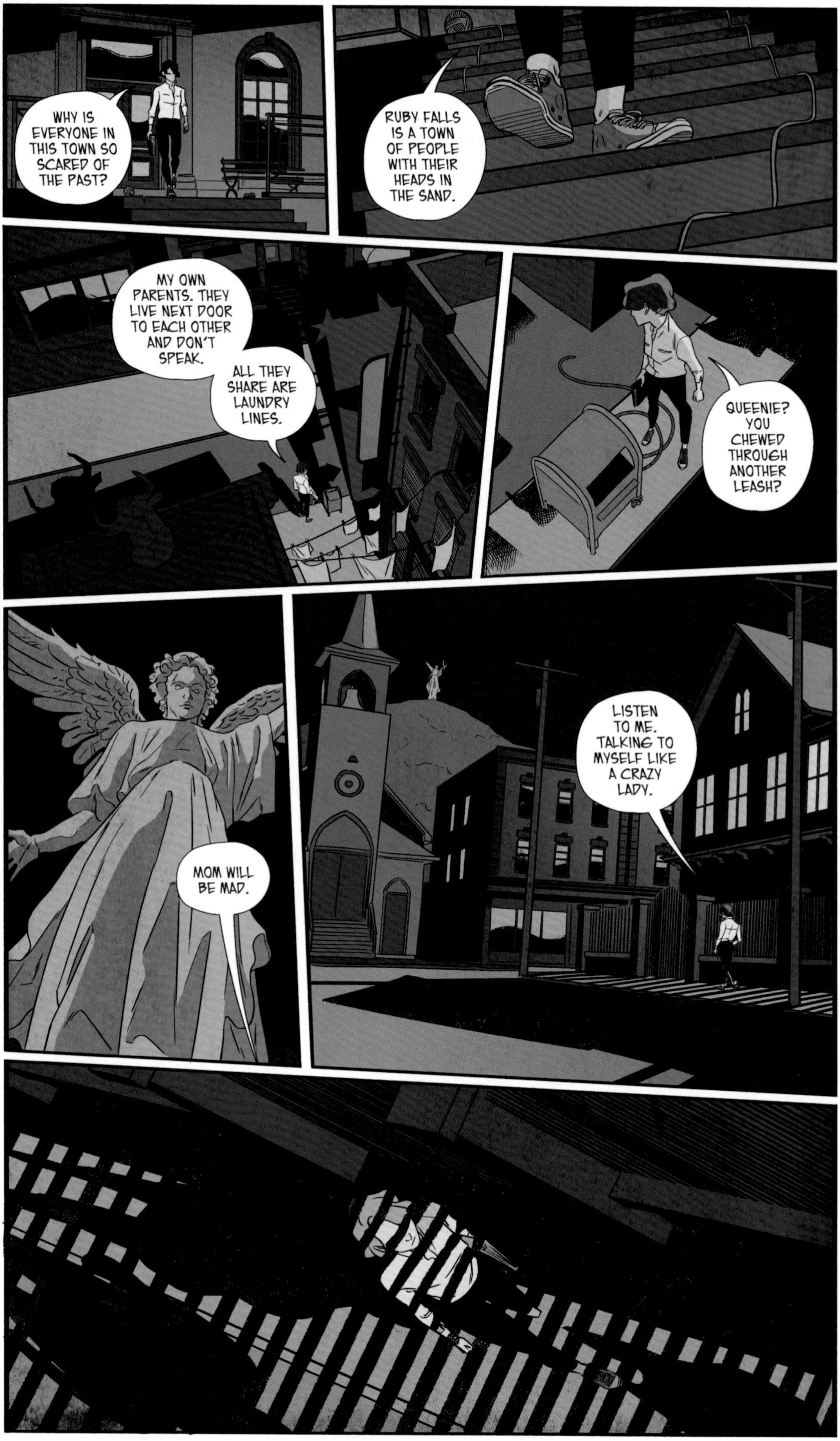
WHY IS EVERYONE IN THIS TOWN SO SCARED OF THE PAST?
RUBY FALLS IS A TOWN OF PEOPLE WITH THEIR HEADS IN THE SAND.
MY OWN PARENTS. THEY LIVE NEXT DOOR TO EACH OTHER AND DON'T SPEAK.
ALL THEY SHARE ARE LAUNDRY LINES.
QUEENIE? YOU CHEWED THROUGH ANOTHER LEASH?
MOM WILL BE MAD.
LISTEN TO ME. TALKING TO MYSELF LIKE A CRAZY LADY.

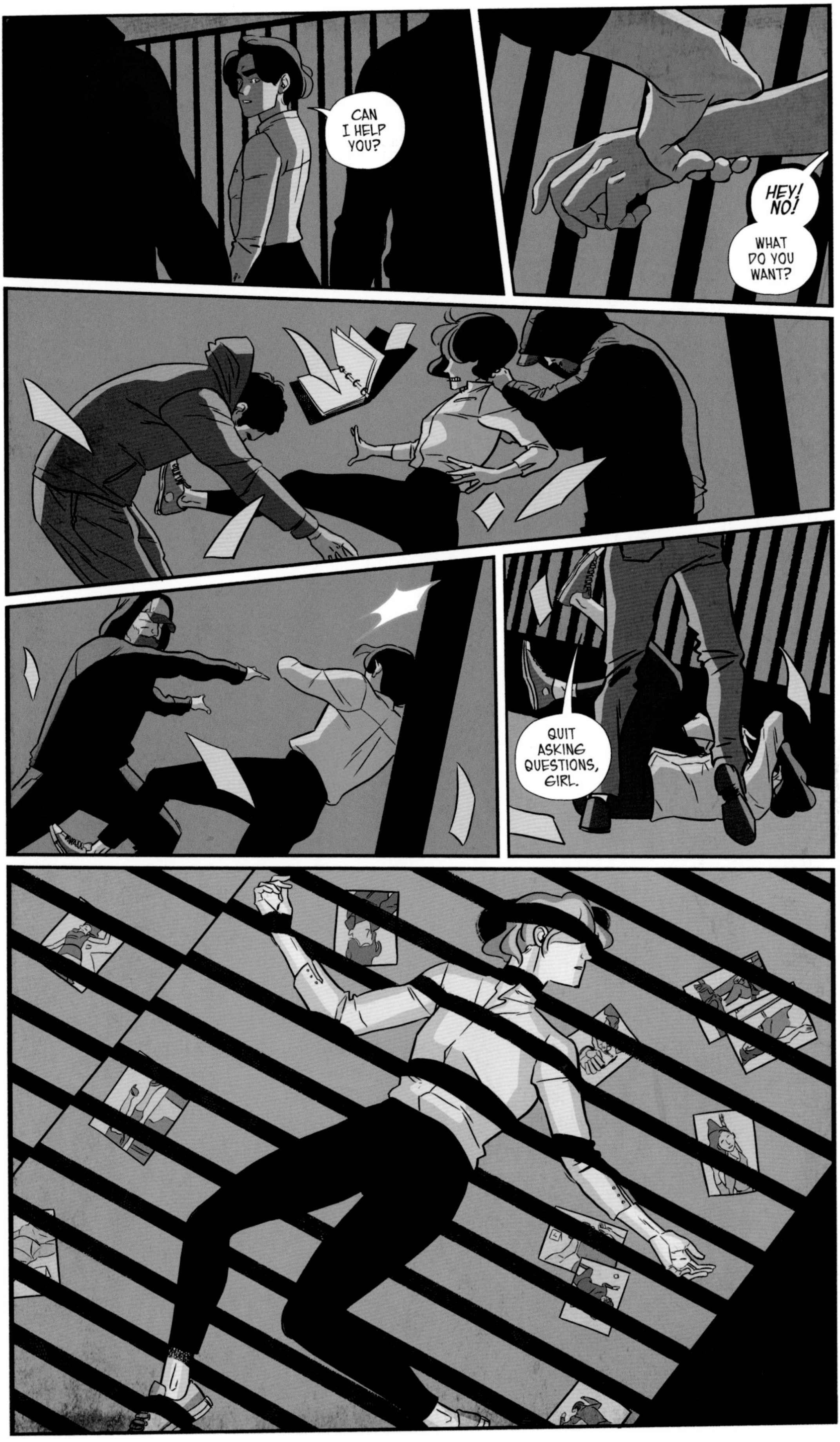
CAN I HELP YOU?
HEY! NO!
WHAT DO YOU WANT?
QUIT ASKING QUESTIONS, GIRL.

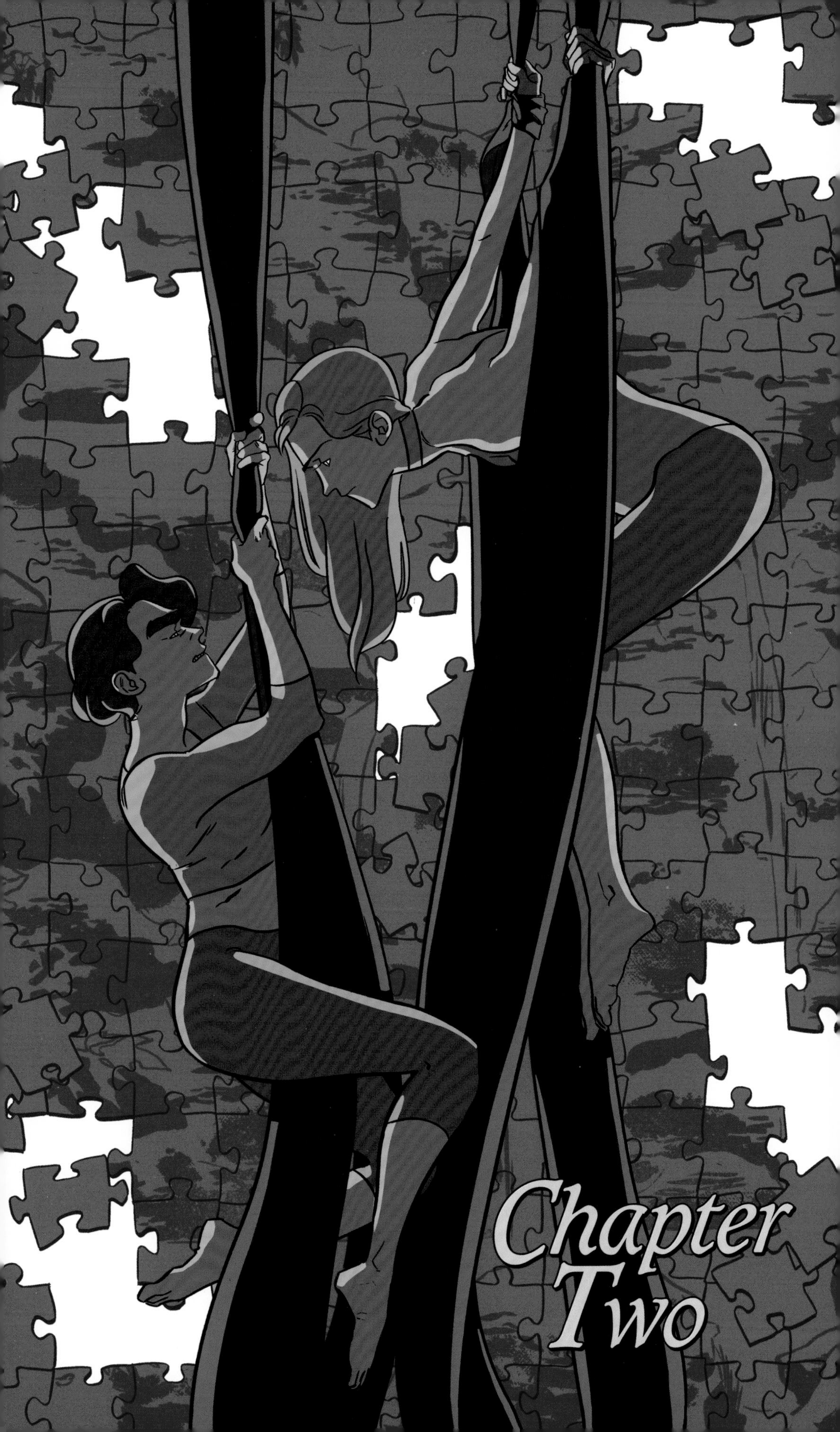
Chapter
Two

" Don't put all

your eggs in

one bastard. "

~DOROTHY PARKER

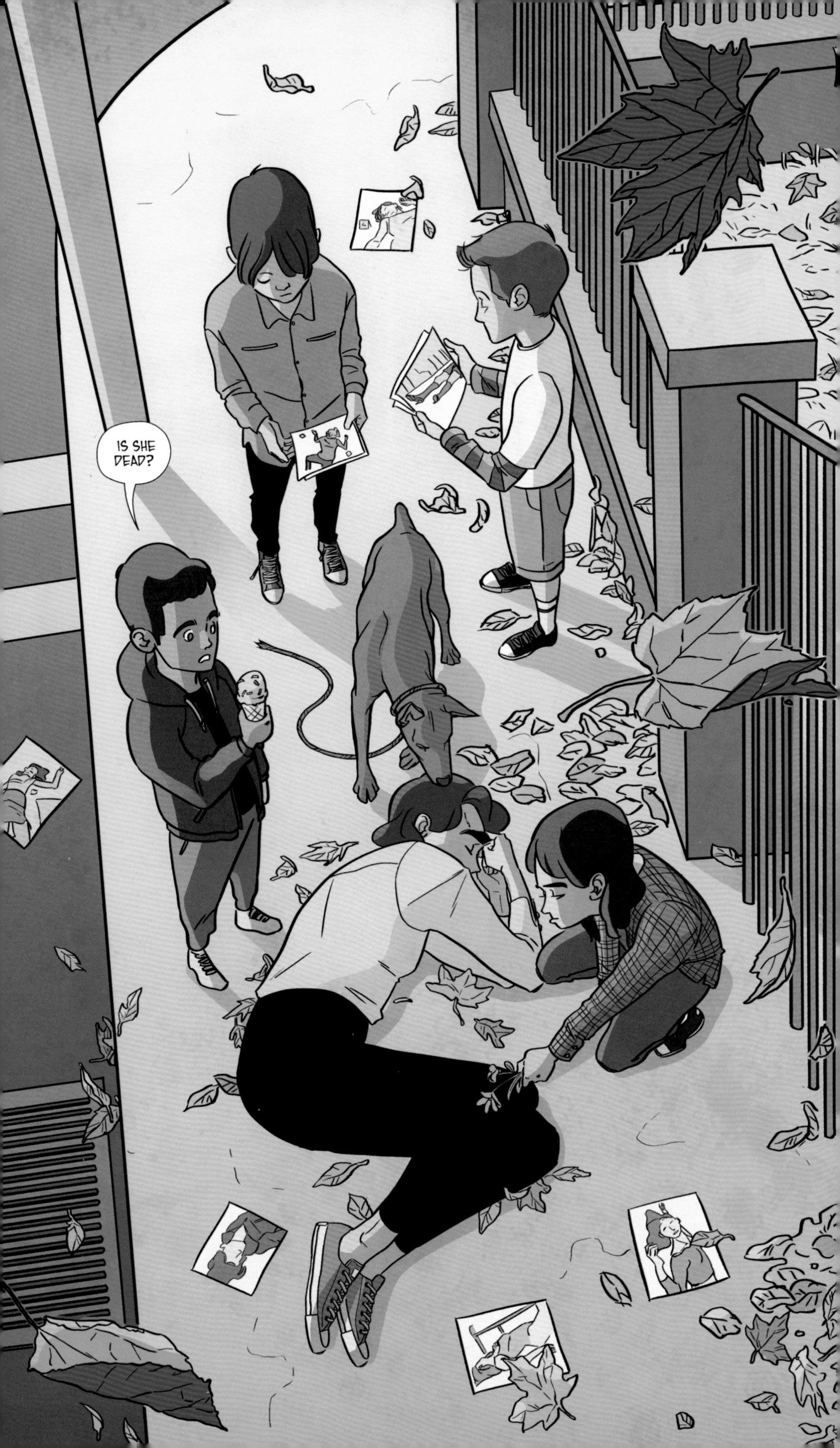
IS SHE DEAD?

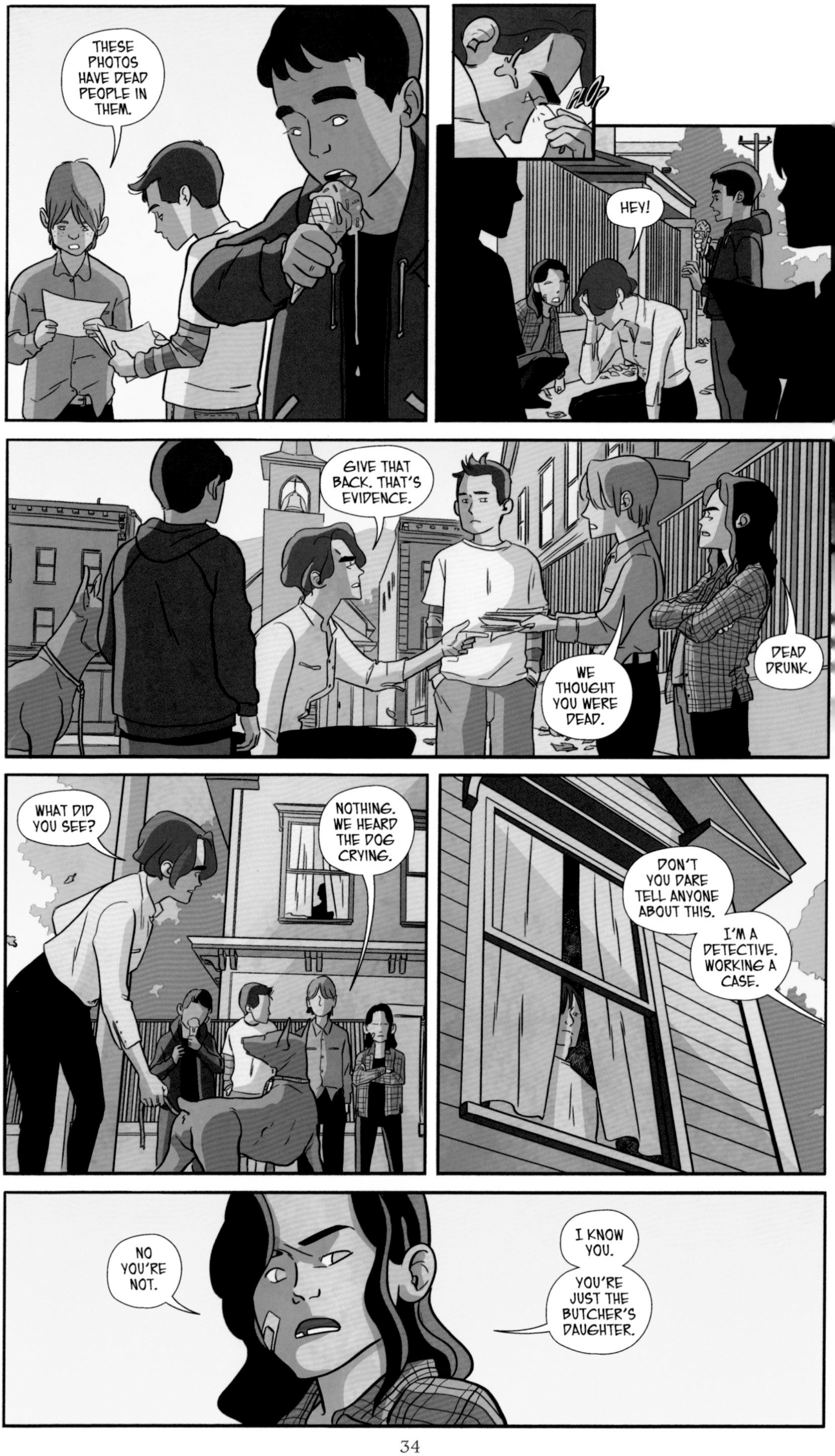
THESE PHOTOS HAVE DEAD PEOPLE IN THEM.
PLOP
HEY!
GIVE THAT BACK. THAT'S EVIDENCE.
WE THOUGHT YOU WERE DEAD.
DEAD DRUNK.
WHAT DID YOU SEE?
NOTHING. WE HEARD THE DOG CRYING.
DON'T YOU DARE TELL ANYONE ABOUT THIS.
I'M A DETECTIVE. WORKING A CASE.
NO YOU'RE NOT.
I KNOW YOU.
YOU'RE JUST THE BUTCHER'S DAUGHTER.

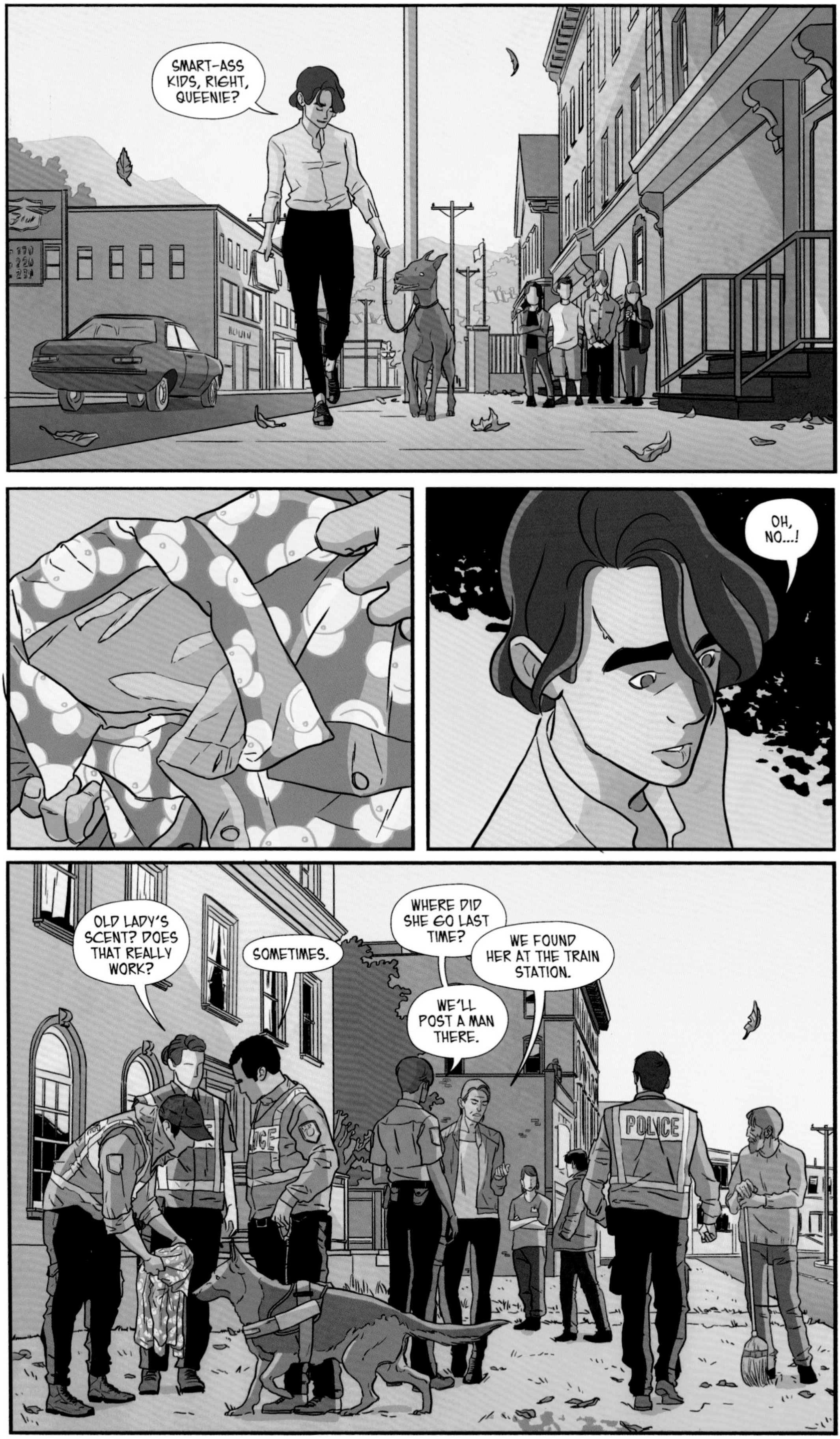
SMART-ASS KIDS, RIGHT, QUEENIE?
OH, NO...!
OLD LADY'S SCENT? DOES THAT REALLY WORK?
SOMETIMES.
WHERE DID SHE GO LAST TIME?
WE FOUND HER AT THE TRAIN STATION.
WE'LL POST A MAN THERE.
POLICE

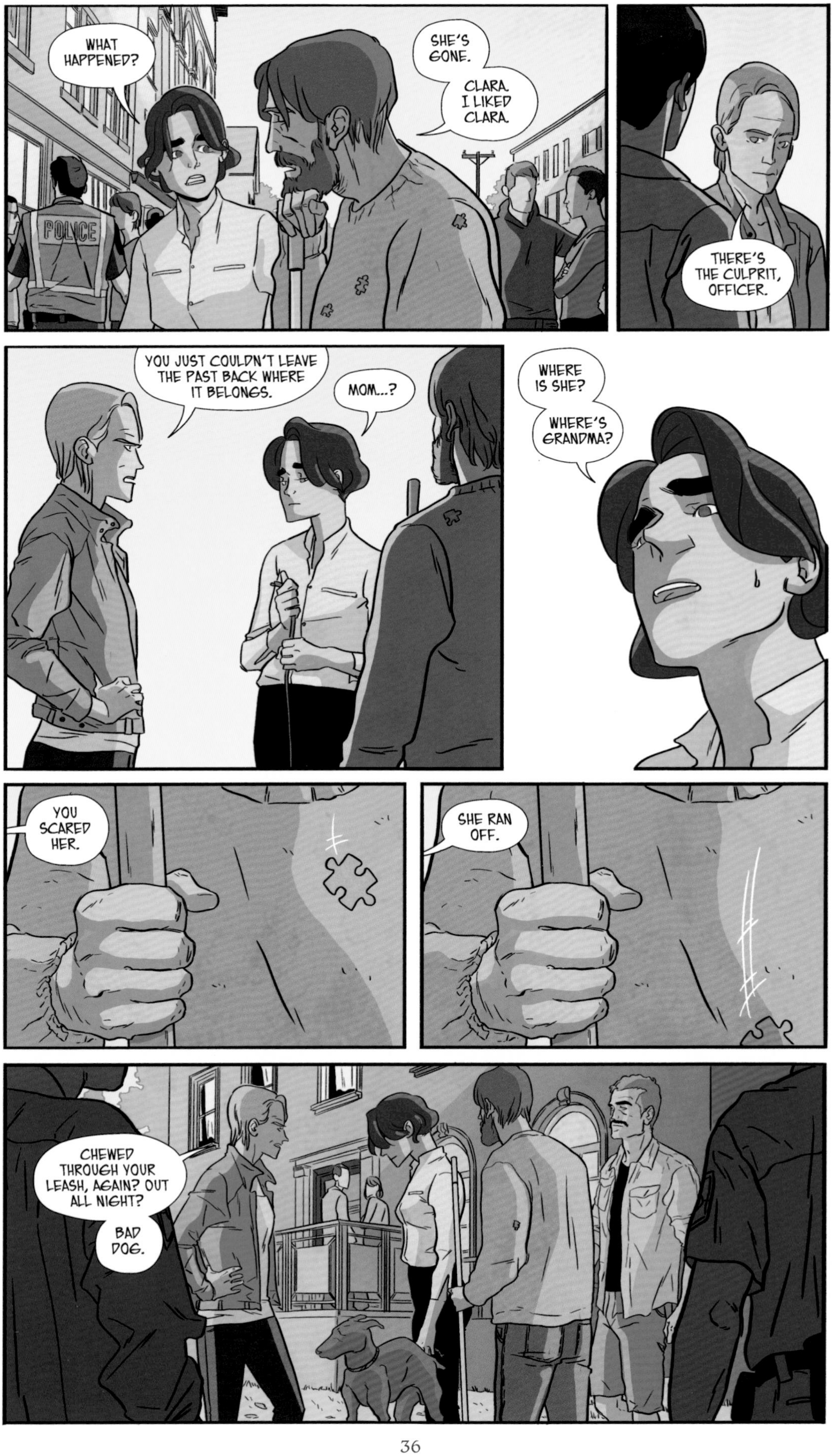
WHAT HAPPENED?
SHE'S GONE.
CLARA. I LIKED CLARA.
THERE'S THE CULPRIT, OFFICER.
YOU JUST COULDN'T LEAVE THE PAST BACK WHERE IT BELONGS.
MOM...?
WHERE IS SHE?
WHERE'S GRANDMA?
YOU SCARED HER.
SHE RAN OFF.
CHEWED THROUGH YOUR LEASH, AGAIN? OUT ALL NIGHT?
BAD DOG.

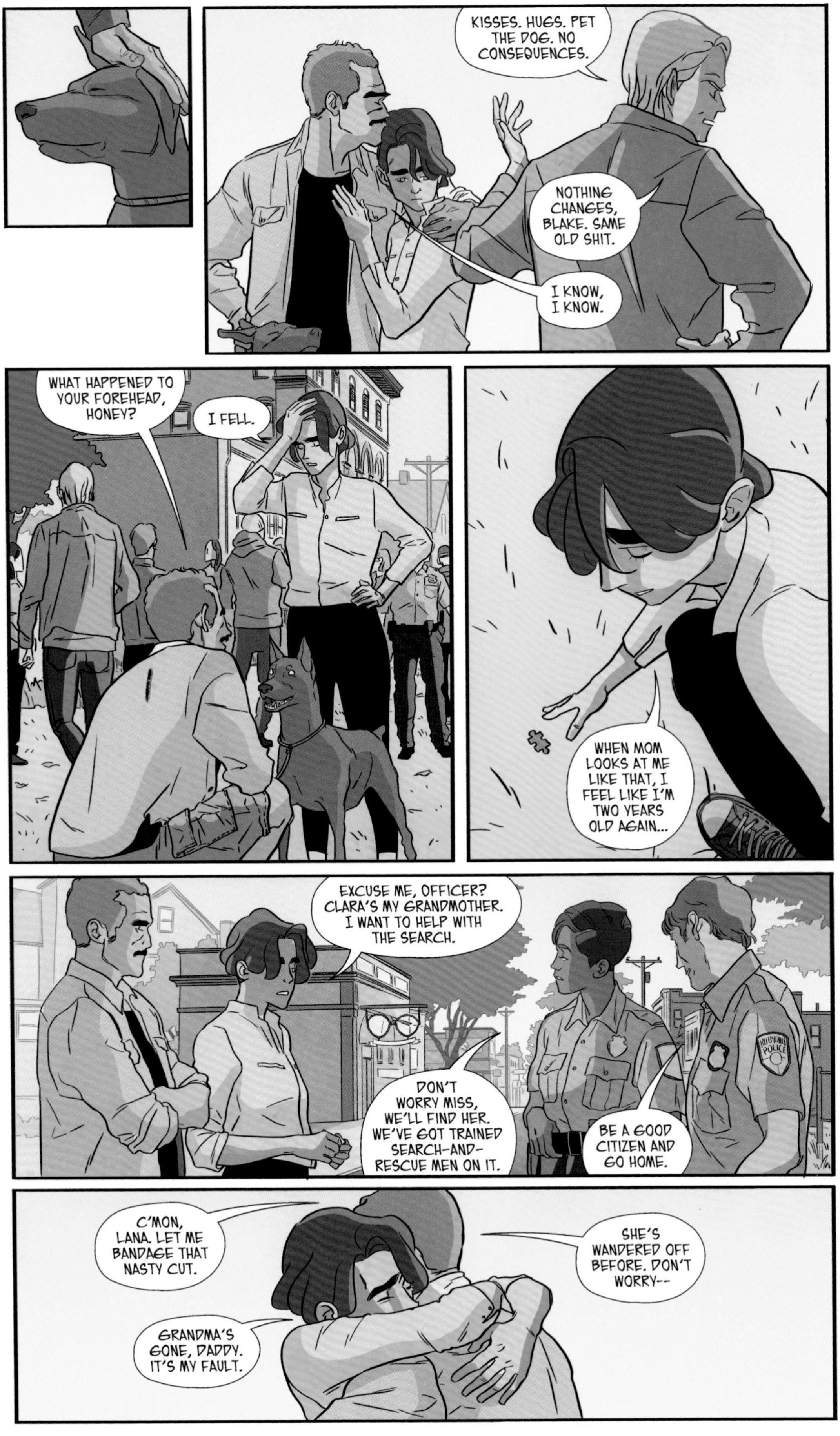
KISSES. HUGS. PET THE DOG. NO CONSEQUENCES.
NOTHING CHANGES, BLAKE. SAME OLD SHIT.
I KNOW, I KNOW.
WHAT HAPPENED TO YOUR FOREHEAD, HONEY?
I FELL.
WHEN MOM LOOKS AT ME LIKE THAT, I FEEL LIKE I'M TWO YEARS OLD AGAIN...
EXCUSE ME, OFFICER? CLARA'S MY GRANDMOTHER. I WANT TO HELP WITH THE SEARCH.
DON'T WORRY MISS, WE'LL FIND HER. WE'VE GOT TRAINED SEARCH-AND-RESCUE MEN ON IT.
BE A GOOD CITIZEN AND GO HOME.
C'MON, LANA. LET ME BANDAGE THAT NASTY CUT.
SHE'S WANDERED OFF BEFORE. DON'T WORRY--
GRANDMA'S GONE, DADDY. IT'S MY FAULT.

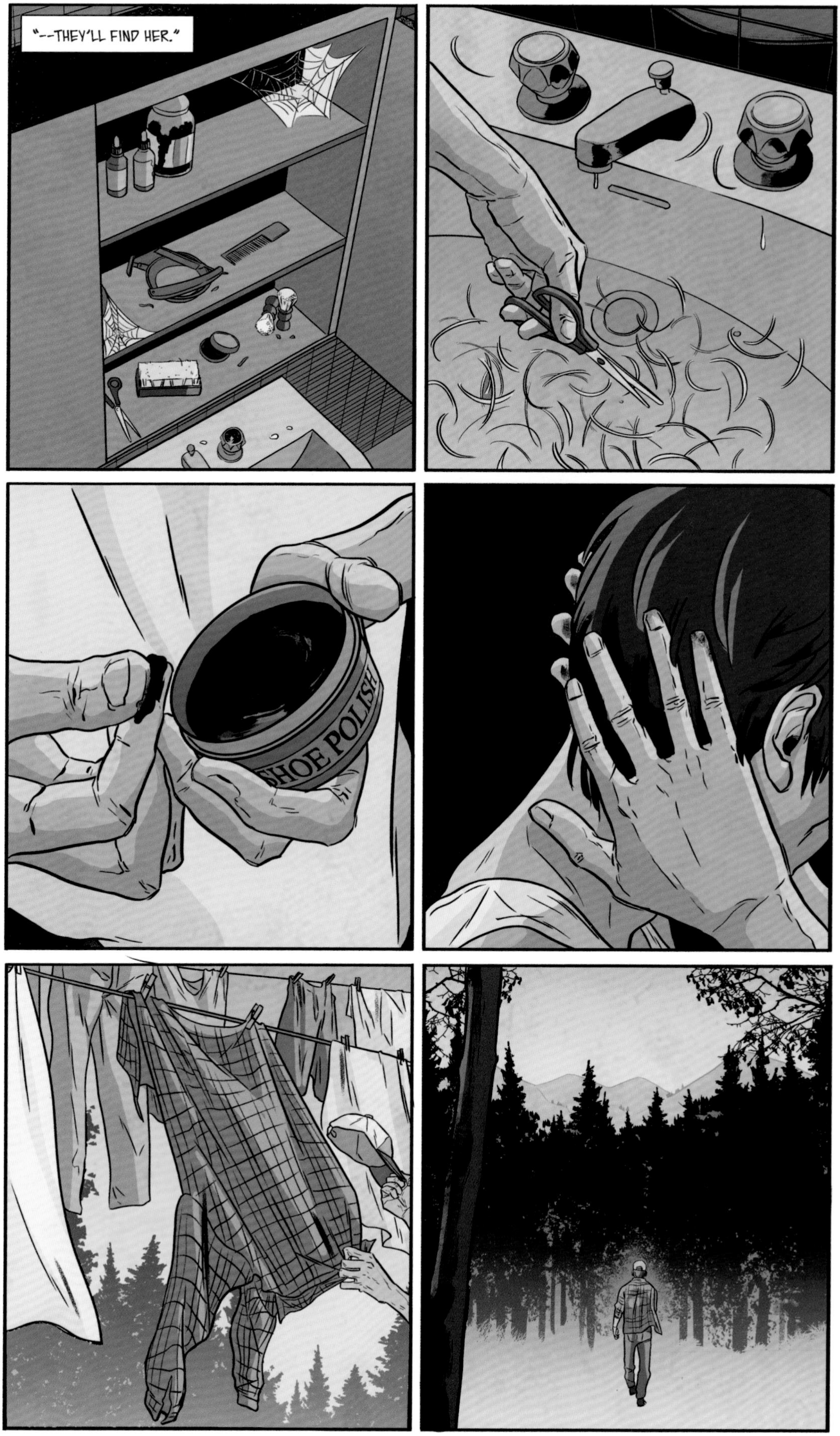
"--THEY'LL FIND HER."
SHOE POLISH

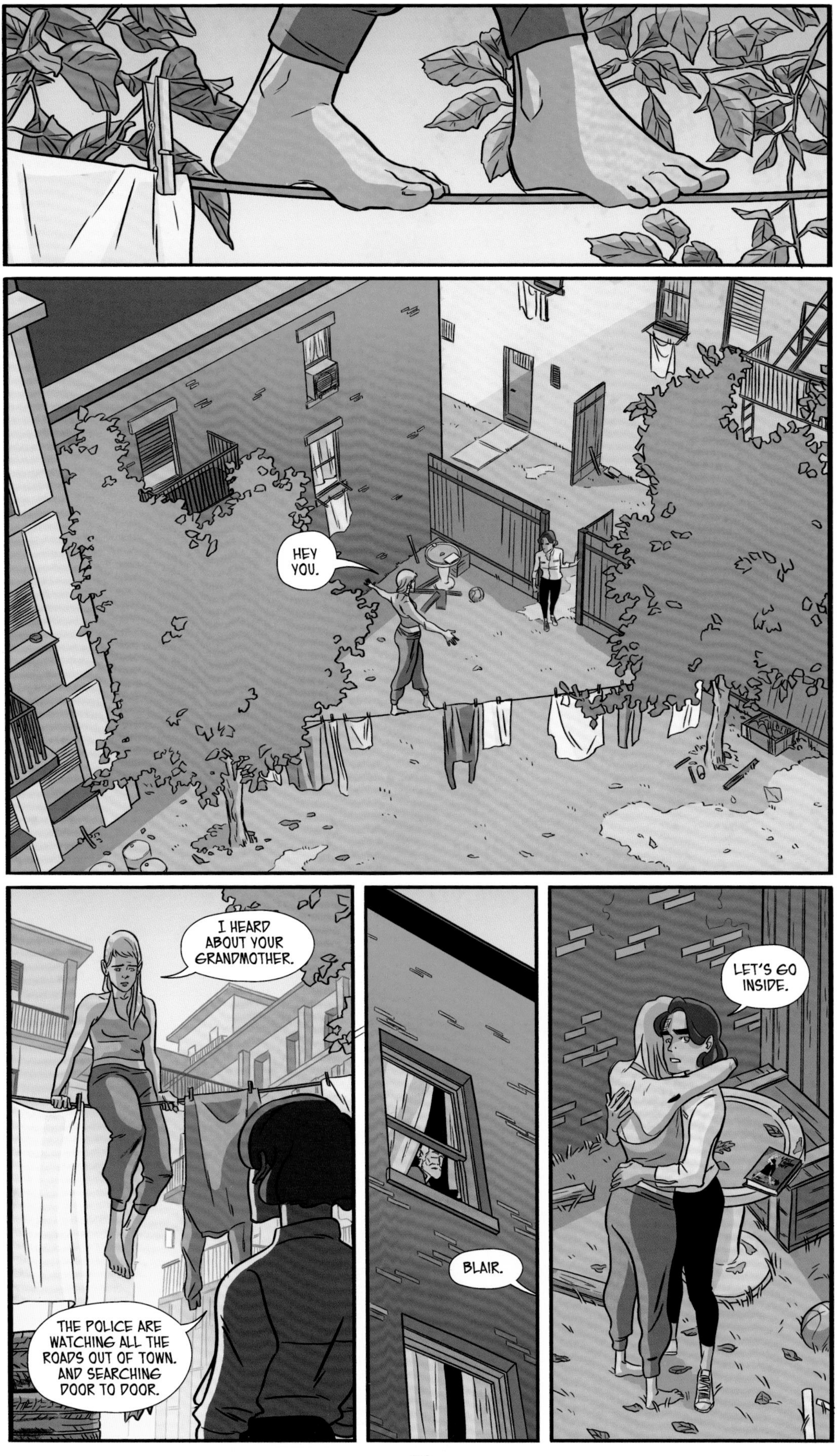
HEY YOU.
I HEARD ABOUT YOUR GRANDMOTHER.
THE POLICE ARE WATCHING ALL THE ROADS OUT OF TOWN. AND SEARCHING DOOR TO DOOR.
BLAIR.
LET'S GO INSIDE.

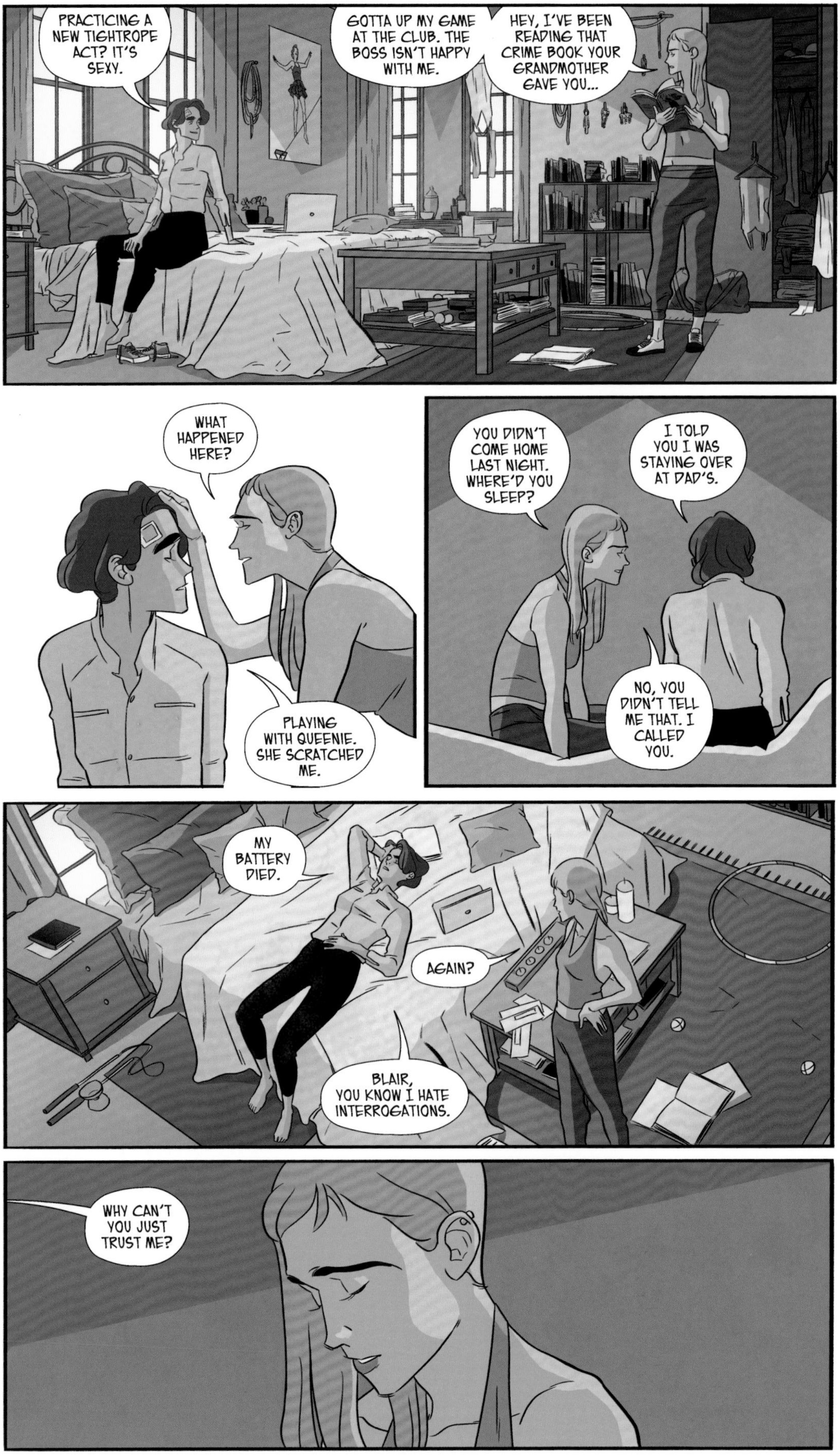
PRACTICING A NEW TIGHTROPE ACT? IT'S SEXY.
GOTTA UP MY GAME AT THE CLUB. THE BOSS ISN'T HAPPY WITH ME.
HEY, I'VE BEEN READING THAT CRIME BOOK YOUR GRANDMOTHER GAVE YOU...
WHAT HAPPENED HERE?
PLAYING WITH QUEENIE. SHE SCRATCHED ME.
YOU DIDN'T COME HOME LAST NIGHT. WHERE'D YOU SLEEP?
I TOLD YOU I WAS STAYING OVER AT DAD'S.
NO, YOU DIDN'T TELL ME THAT. I CALLED YOU.
MY BATTERY DIED.
AGAIN?
BLAIR, YOU KNOW I HATE INTERROGATIONS.
WHY CAN'T YOU JUST TRUST ME?

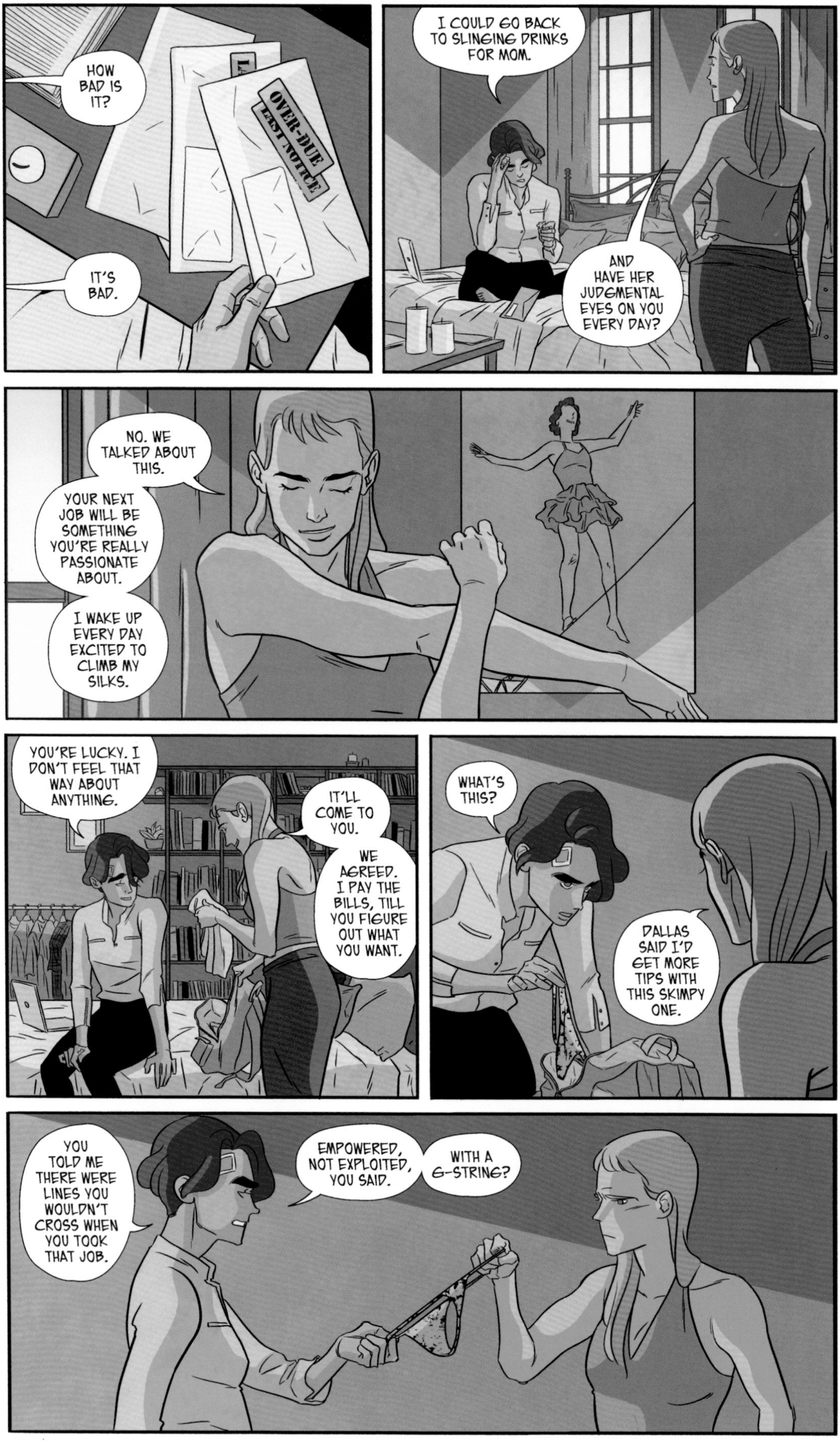
HOW BAD IS IT?
OVER-DUE
LAST NOTICE
IT'S BAD.
I COULD GO BACK TO SLINGING DRINKS FOR MOM.
AND HAVE HER JUDGEMENTAL EYES ON YOU EVERY DAY?
NO. WE TALKED ABOUT THIS.
YOUR NEXT JOB WILL BE SOMETHING YOU'RE REALLY PASSIONATE ABOUT.
I WAKE UP EVERY DAY EXCITED TO CLIMB MY SILKS.
YOU'RE LUCKY. I DON'T FEEL THAT WAY ABOUT ANYTHING.
IT'LL COME TO YOU.
WE AGREED. I PAY THE BILLS, TILL YOU FIGURE OUT WHAT YOU WANT.
WHAT'S THIS?
DALLAS SAID I'D GET MORE TIPS WITH THIS SKIMPY ONE.
YOU TOLD ME THERE WERE LINES YOU WOULDN'T CROSS WHEN YOU TOOK THAT JOB.
EMPOWERED, NOT EXPLOITED, YOU SAID.
WITH A G-STRING?

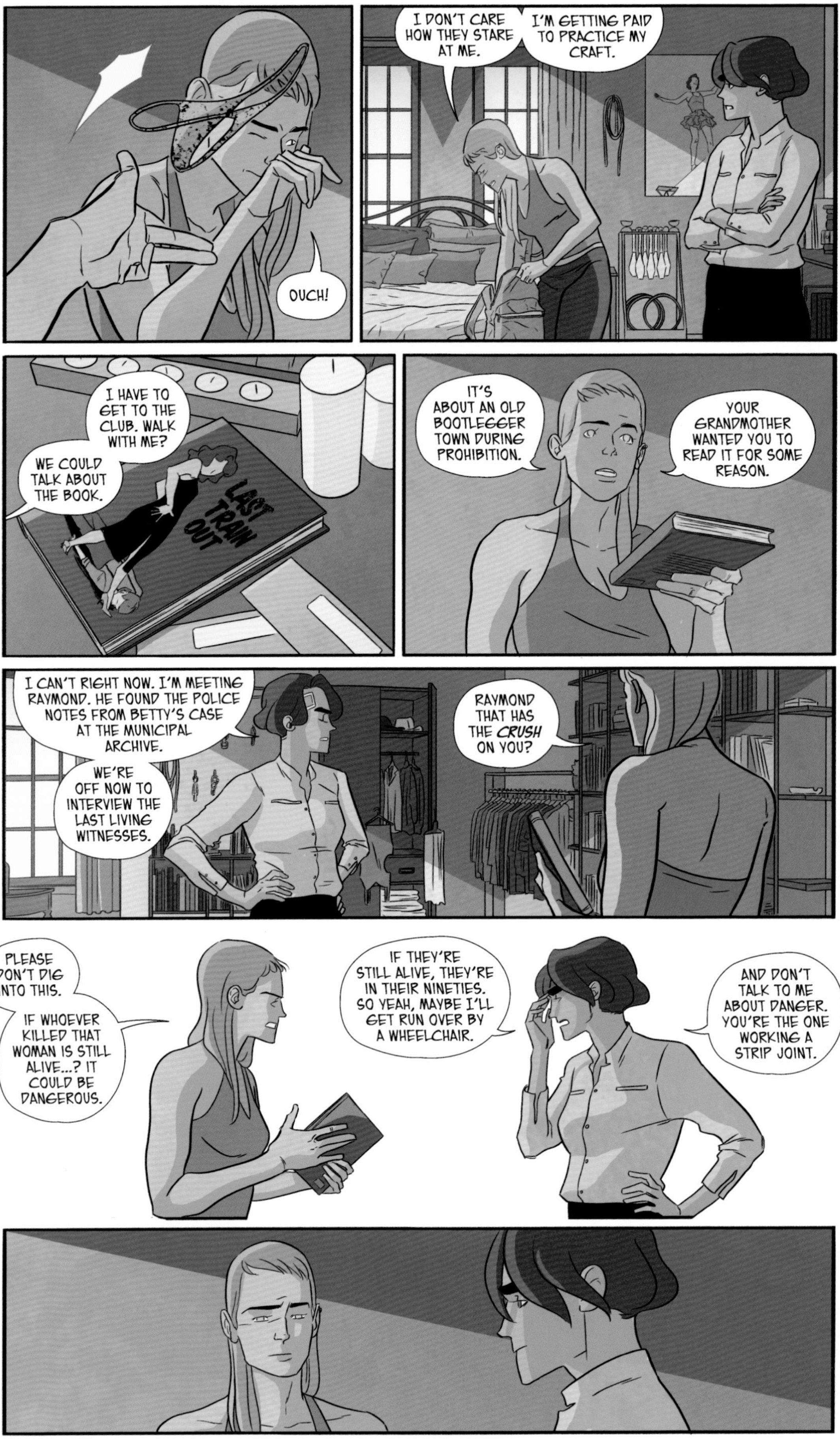
OUCH!
I DON'T CARE HOW THEY STARE AT ME.
I'M GETTING PAID TO PRACTICE MY CRAFT.
I HAVE TO GET TO THE CLUB. WALK WITH ME?
WE COULD TALK ABOUT THE BOOK.
LAST TRAIN OUT
IT'S ABOUT AN OLD BOOTLEGGER TOWN DURING PROHIBITION.
YOUR GRANDMOTHER WANTED YOU TO READ IT FOR SOME REASON.
I CAN'T RIGHT NOW. I'M MEETING RAYMOND. HE FOUND THE POLICE NOTES FROM BETTY'S CASE AT THE MUNICIPAL ARCHIVE.
WE'RE OFF NOW TO INTERVIEW THE LAST LIVING WITNESSES.
RAYMOND THAT HAS THE *CRUSH* ON YOU?
PLEASE DON'T DIG INTO THIS.
IF WHOEVER KILLED THAT WOMAN IS STILL ALIVE...? IT COULD BE DANGEROUS.
IF THEY'RE STILL ALIVE, THEY'RE IN THEIR NINETIES. SO YEAH, MAYBE I'LL GET RUN OVER BY A WHEELCHAIR.
AND DON'T TALK TO ME ABOUT DANGER. YOU'RE THE ONE WORKING A STRIP JOINT.

THIS IS IT. WHERE THE MINERS LIVED, BACK IN THE '30S. IT WAS A ROUGH STREET, ALL BARS AND BROTHELS.

SOUNDS FUN. AND YOUR LITTLE MAP IS CUTE, RAYMOND.

MINING CAVES

MAIN STREET

I WAS HOPING YOU'D LIKE IT.

I LOVE IT.

THE POLICE NOTES SHOW MULTIPLE SUSPECTS, LOTS OF ALIBIS. THIS CASE WENT COLD FAST. TOO FAST.

THE HOUSING REGISTER INDICATED ONLY ONE HOUSE STILL HAS THE ORIGINAL OWNER AS BACK THEN.

NO BODY, NO WEAPON, NO WITNESSES. HARD TO MAKE A MURDER CHARGE STICK WITHOUT THOSE THINGS.

WE'RE STARTING OFF WITH DEAD ENDS.

MISSING

HAVE YOU SEEN THIS WOMAN?

I WARNED YOU IT WOULD BE FRUSTRATING. YOU CAN WORK AN OLD CASE AND EVENTUALLY FIND VESTIGIAL TRACES OF A CRIME, GHOST FOOTPRINTS FROM THE PAST—

—BUT IT'S RARE, SOLVING A CASE THAT'S GONE THIS COLD.

I HAVE TO MAKE THE FIRST MOVE?

IT'S YOUR PARTY.

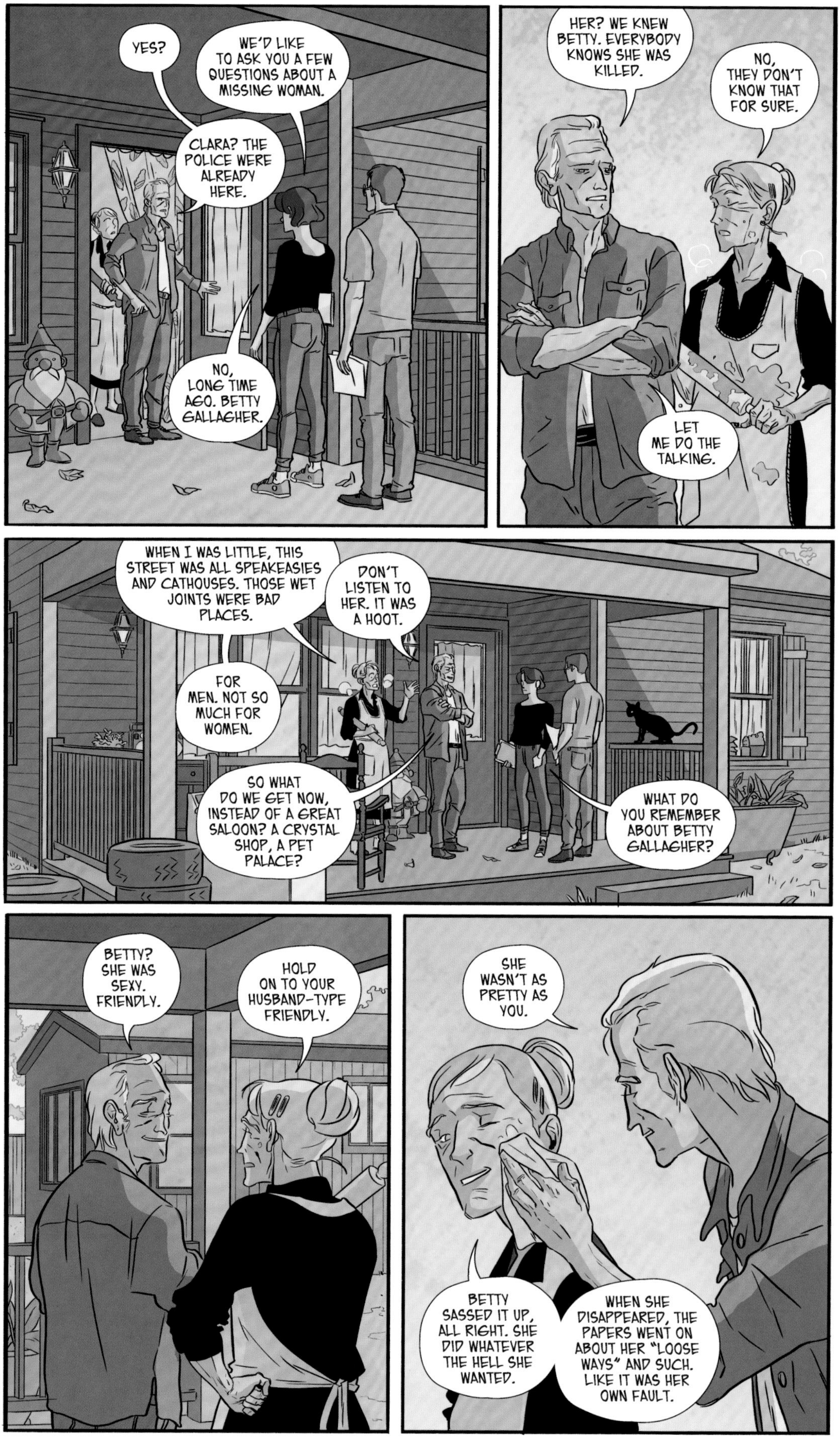
YES?
WE'D LIKE TO ASK YOU A FEW QUESTIONS ABOUT A MISSING WOMAN.
CLARA? THE POLICE WERE ALREADY HERE.
NO, LONG TIME AGO. BETTY GALLAGHER.
HER? WE KNEW BETTY. EVERYBODY KNOWS SHE WAS KILLED.
NO, THEY DON'T KNOW THAT FOR SURE.
LET ME DO THE TALKING.
WHEN I WAS LITTLE, THIS STREET WAS ALL SPEAKEASIES AND CATHOUSES. THOSE WET JOINTS WERE BAD PLACES.
DON'T LISTEN TO HER. IT WAS A HOOT.
FOR MEN. NOT SO MUCH FOR WOMEN.
SO WHAT DO WE GET NOW, INSTEAD OF A GREAT SALOON? A CRYSTAL SHOP, A PET PALACE?
WHAT DO YOU REMEMBER ABOUT BETTY GALLAGHER?
BETTY? SHE WAS SEXY. FRIENDLY.
HOLD ON TO YOUR HUSBAND-TYPE FRIENDLY.
SHE WASN'T AS PRETTY AS YOU.
BETTY SASSED IT UP, ALL RIGHT. SHE DID WHATEVER THE HELL SHE WANTED.
WHEN SHE DISAPPEARED, THE PAPERS WENT ON ABOUT HER "LOOSE WAYS" AND SUCH. LIKE IT WAS HER OWN FAULT.

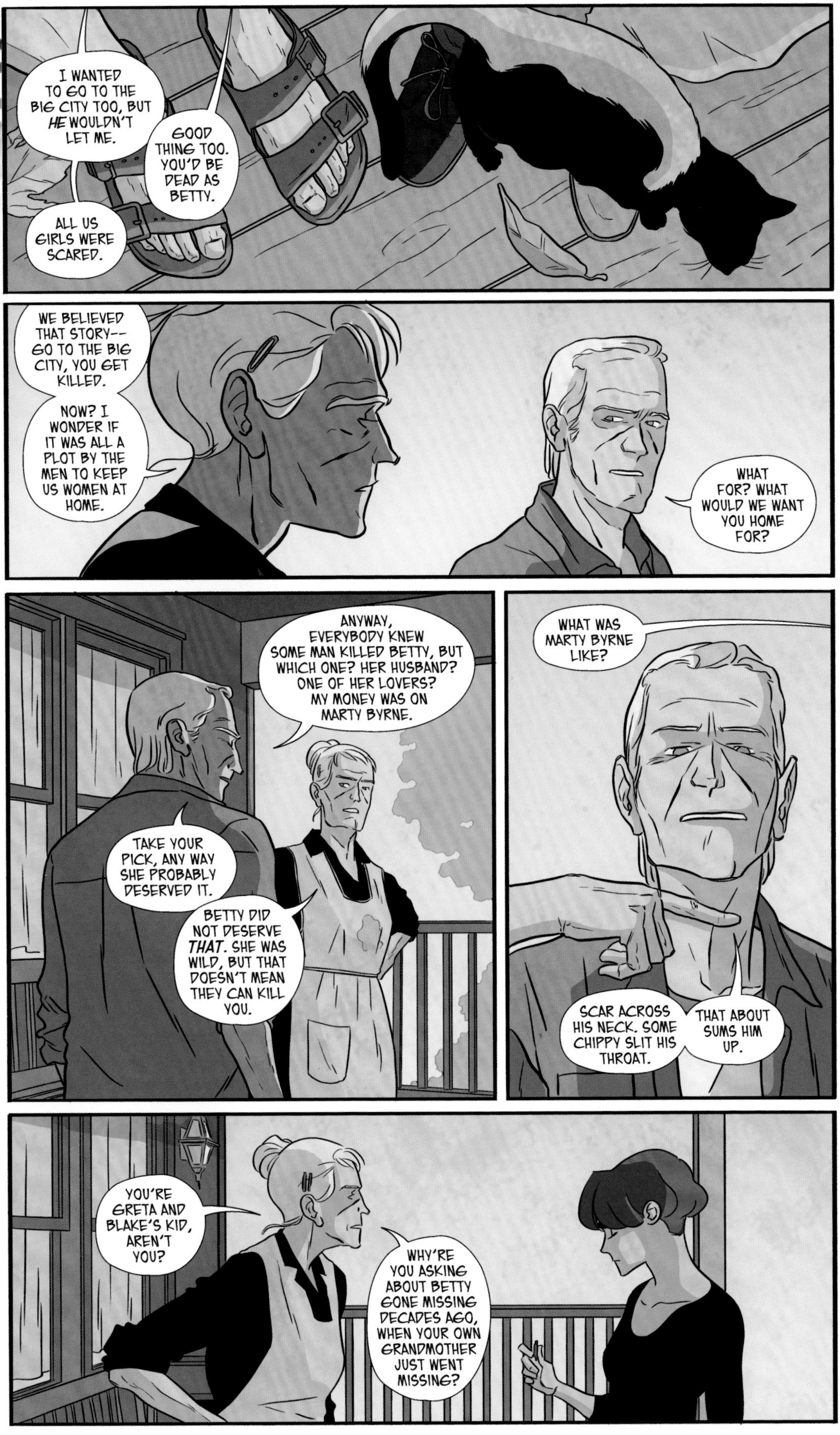
I WANTED TO GO TO THE BIG CITY TOO, BUT *HE* WOULDN'T LET ME.
ALL US GIRLS WERE SCARED.
GOOD THING TOO. YOU'D BE DEAD AS BETTY.
WE BELIEVED THAT STORY-- GO TO THE BIG CITY, YOU GET KILLED.
NOW? I WONDER IF IT WAS ALL A PLOT BY THE MEN TO KEEP US WOMEN AT HOME.
WHAT FOR? WHAT WOULD WE WANT YOU HOME FOR?
ANYWAY, EVERYBODY KNEW SOME MAN KILLED BETTY, BUT WHICH ONE? HER HUSBAND? ONE OF HER LOVERS? MY MONEY WAS ON MARTY BYRNE.
TAKE YOUR PICK, ANY WAY SHE PROBABLY DESERVED IT.
BETTY DID NOT DESERVE *THAT*. SHE WAS WILD, BUT THAT DOESN'T MEAN THEY CAN KILL YOU.
WHAT WAS MARTY BYRNE LIKE?
SCAR ACROSS HIS NECK. SOME CHIPPY SLIT HIS THROAT.
THAT ABOUT SUMS HIM UP.
YOU'RE GRETA AND BLAKE'S KID, AREN'T YOU?
WHY'RE YOU ASKING ABOUT BETTY GONE MISSING DECADES AGO, WHEN YOUR OWN GRANDMOTHER JUST WENT MISSING?

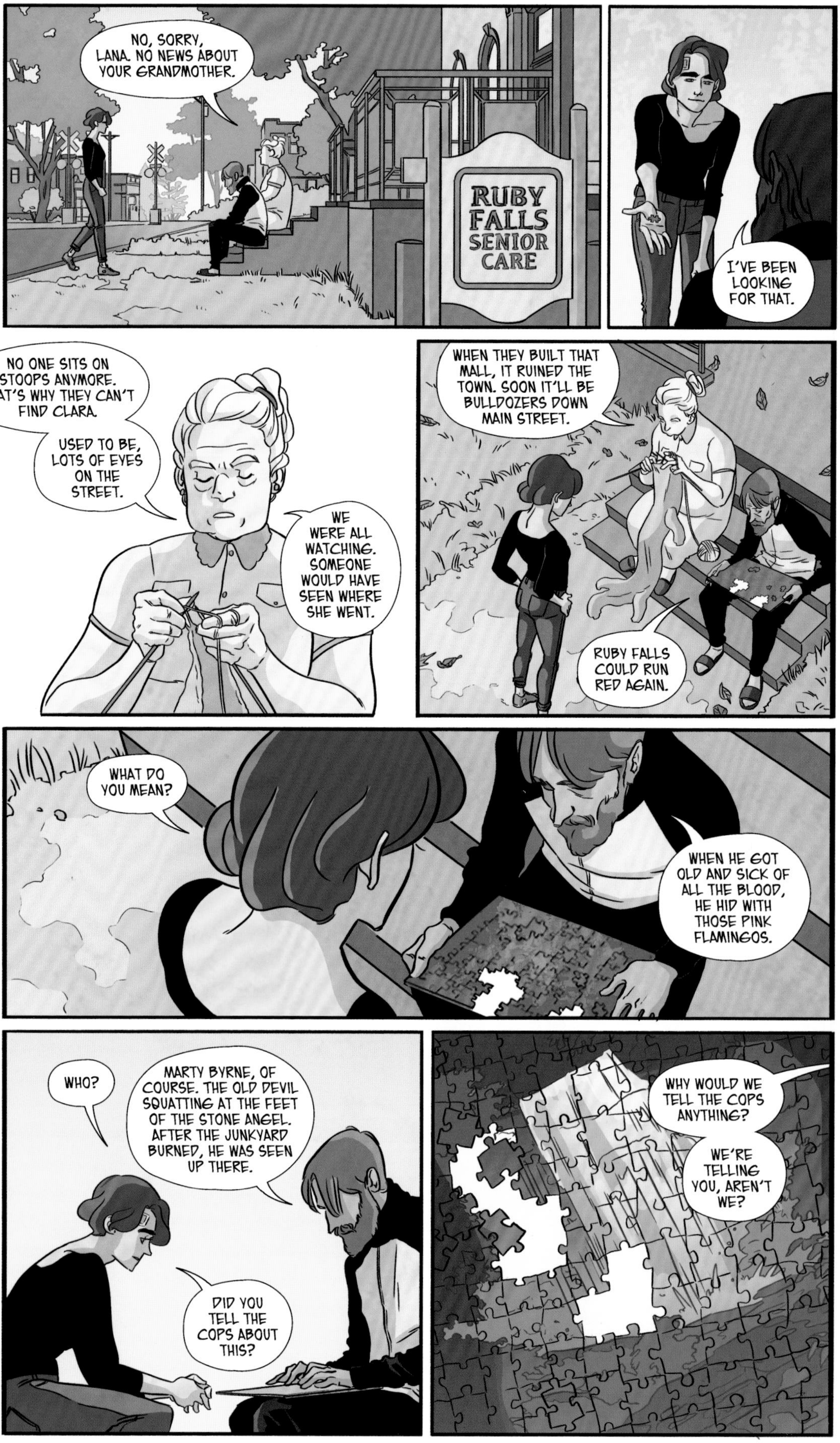
NO, SORRY, LANA. NO NEWS ABOUT YOUR GRANDMOTHER.
RUBY FALLS SENIOR CARE
I'VE BEEN LOOKING FOR THAT.
NO ONE SITS ON STOOPS ANYMORE. THAT'S WHY THEY CAN'T FIND CLARA.
USED TO BE, LOTS OF EYES ON THE STREET.
WE WERE ALL WATCHING. SOMEONE WOULD HAVE SEEN WHERE SHE WENT.
WHEN THEY BUILT THAT MALL, IT RUINED THE TOWN. SOON IT'LL BE BULLDOZERS DOWN MAIN STREET.
RUBY FALLS COULD RUN RED AGAIN.
WHAT DO YOU MEAN?
WHEN HE GOT OLD AND SICK OF ALL THE BLOOD, HE HID WITH THOSE PINK FLAMINGOS.
WHO?
MARTY BYRNE, OF COURSE. THE OLD DEVIL SQUATTING AT THE FEET OF THE STONE ANGEL. AFTER THE JUNKYARD BURNED, HE WAS SEEN UP THERE.
DID YOU TELL THE COPS ABOUT THIS?
WHY WOULD WE TELL THE COPS ANYTHING?
WE'RE TELLING YOU, AREN'T WE?

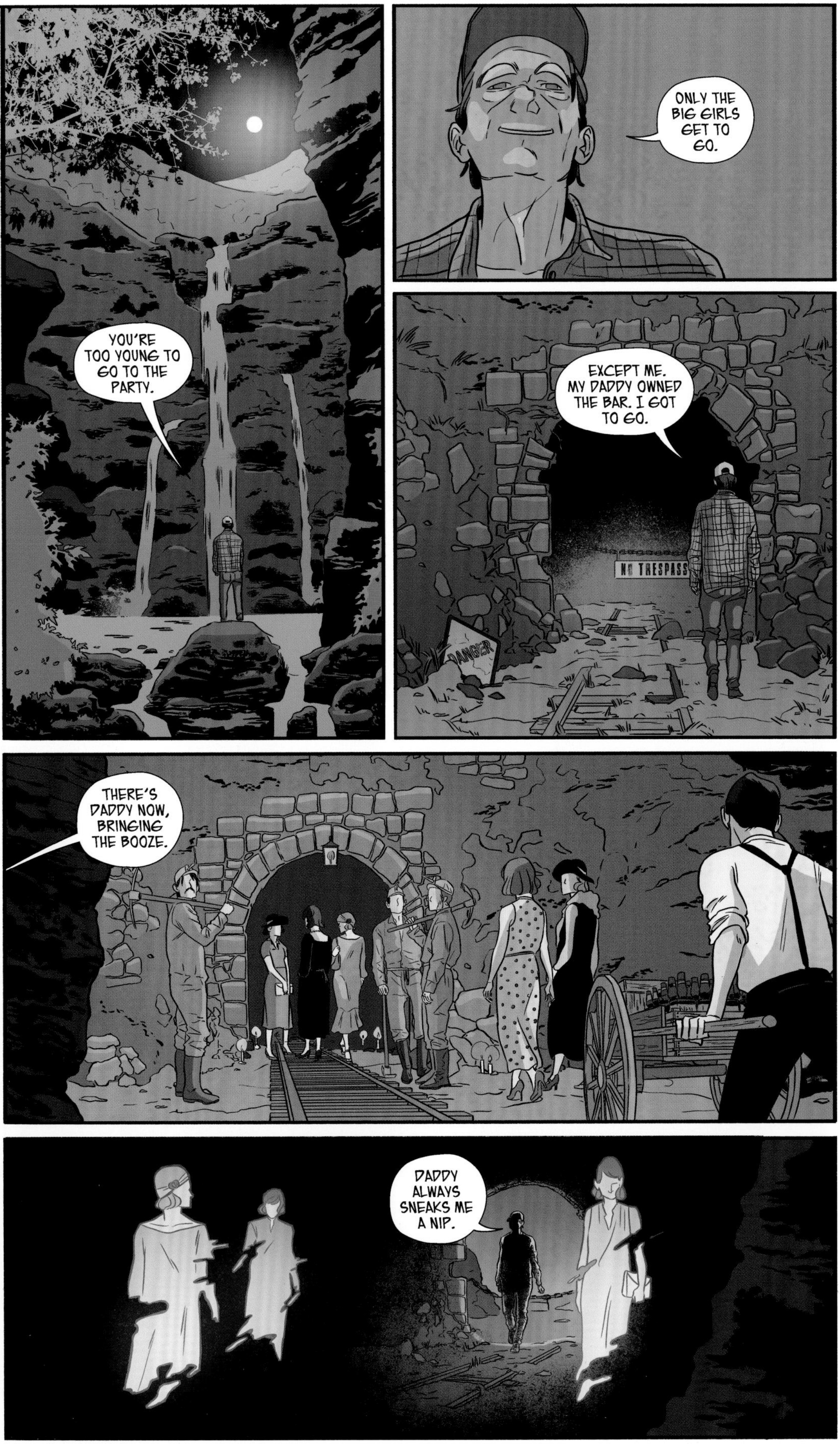
YOU'RE TOO YOUNG TO GO TO THE PARTY.
ONLY THE BIG GIRLS GET TO GO.
EXCEPT ME. MY DADDY OWNED THE BAR. I GOT TO GO.
NO TRESPASS
DANGER
THERE'S DADDY NOW, BRINGING THE BOOZE.
DADDY ALWAYS SNEAKS ME A NIP.

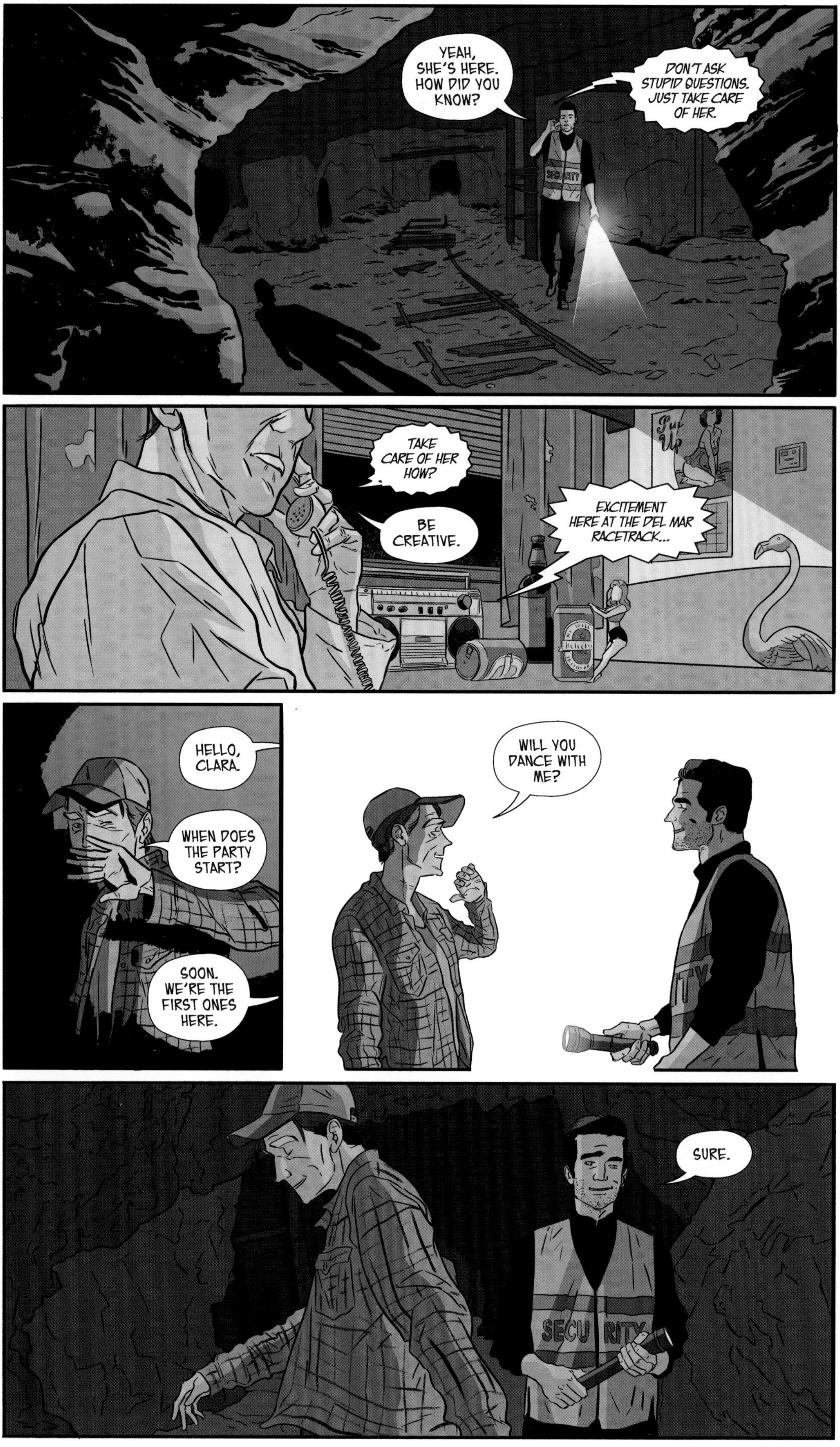
YEAH, SHE'S HERE. HOW DID YOU KNOW?
DON'T ASK STUPID QUESTIONS. JUST TAKE CARE OF HER.
SECURITY
TAKE CARE OF HER HOW?
BE CREATIVE.
EXCITEMENT HERE AT THE DEL MAR RACETRACK...
HELLO, CLARA.
WHEN DOES THE PARTY START?
SOON. WE'RE THE FIRST ONES HERE.
WILL YOU DANCE WITH ME?
SURE.
SECURITY

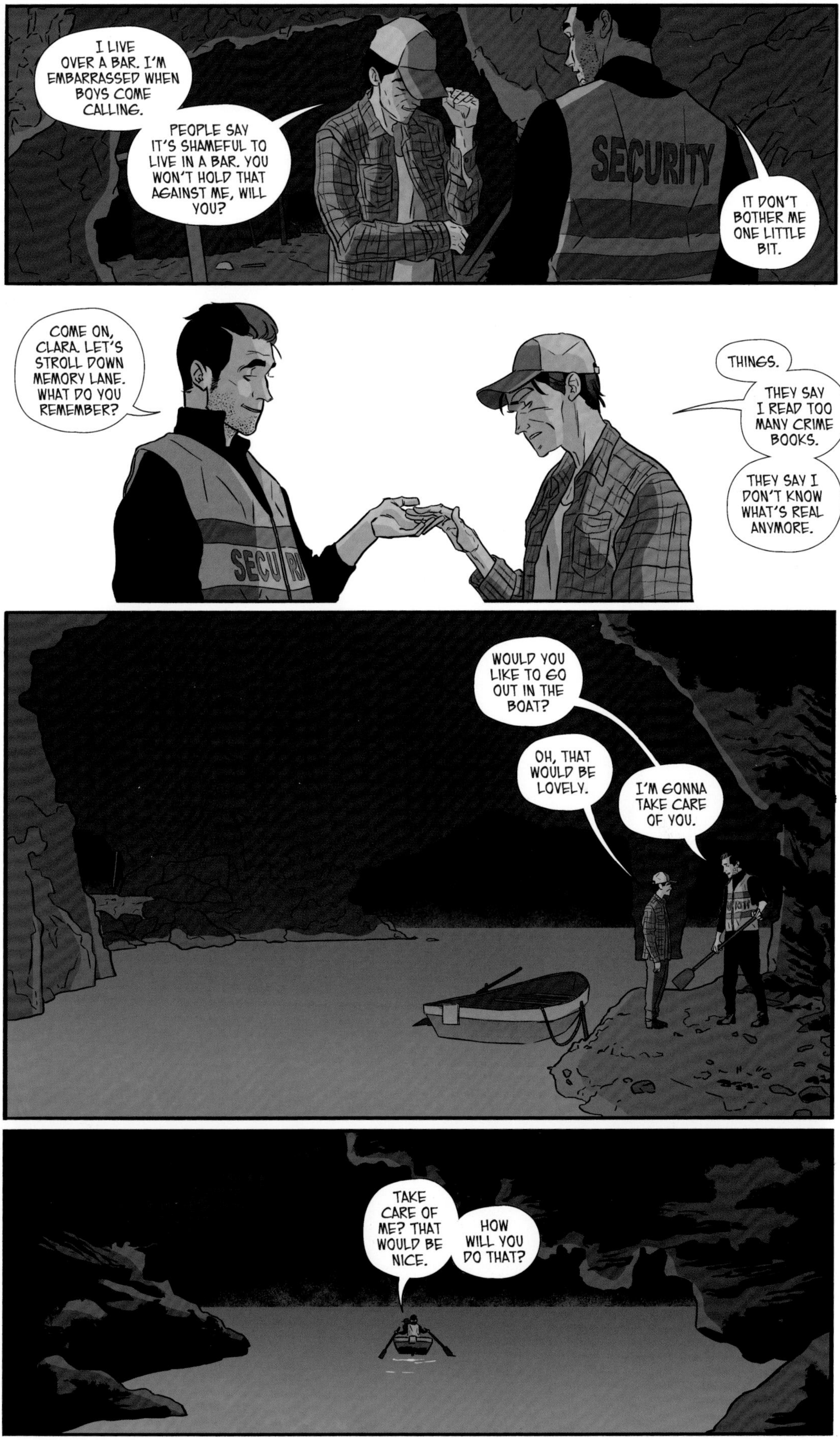
I LIVE OVER A BAR. I'M EMBARRASSED WHEN BOYS COME CALLING.
PEOPLE SAY IT'S SHAMEFUL TO LIVE IN A BAR. YOU WON'T HOLD THAT AGAINST ME, WILL YOU?
SECURITY
IT DON'T BOTHER ME ONE LITTLE BIT.
COME ON, CLARA. LET'S STROLL DOWN MEMORY LANE. WHAT DO YOU REMEMBER?
THINGS.
THEY SAY I READ TOO MANY CRIME BOOKS.
THEY SAY I DON'T KNOW WHAT'S REAL ANYMORE.
WOULD YOU LIKE TO GO OUT IN THE BOAT?
OH, THAT WOULD BE LOVELY.
I'M GONNA TAKE CARE OF YOU.
TAKE CARE OF ME? THAT WOULD BE NICE.
HOW WILL YOU DO THAT?

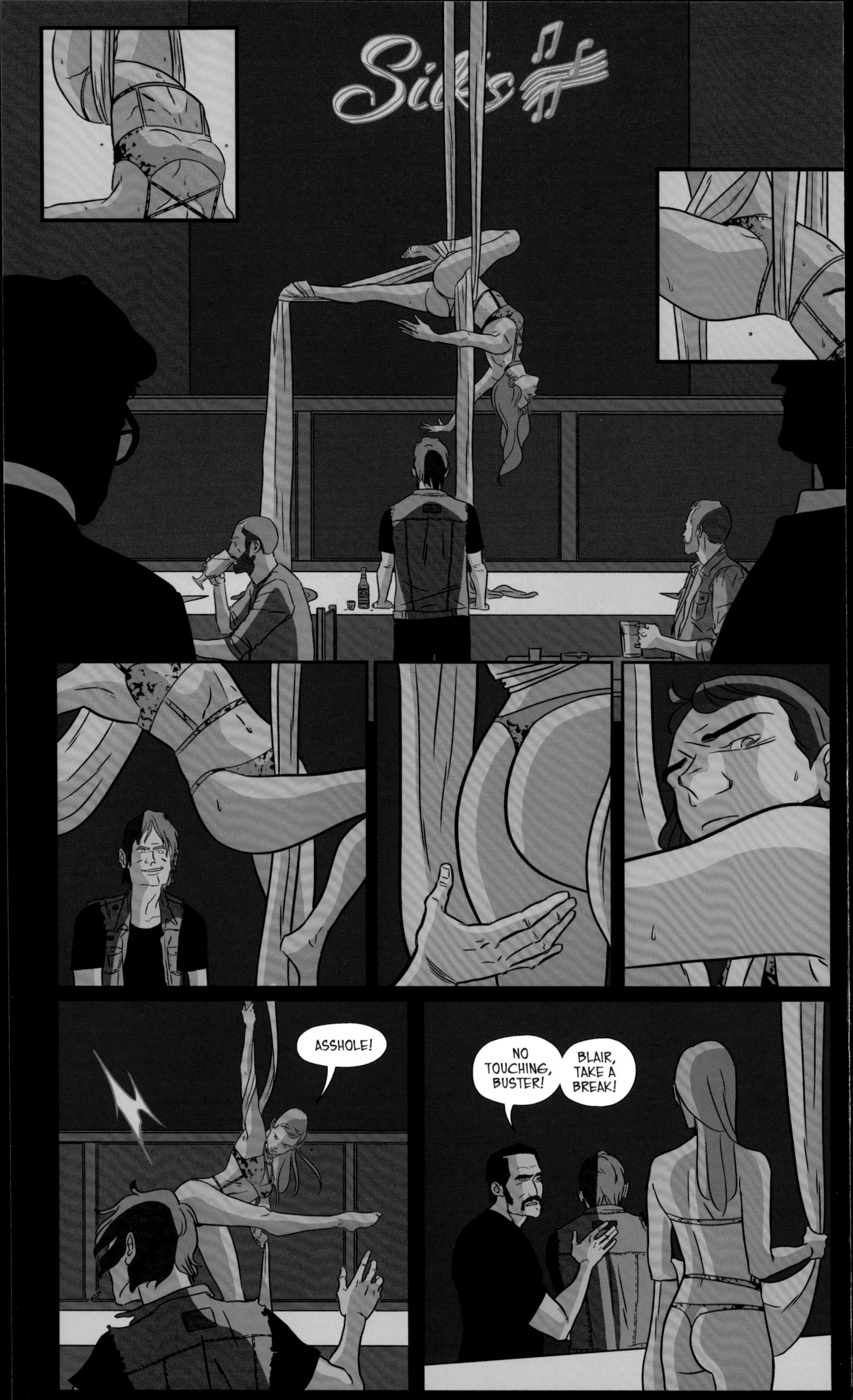

Silks
ASSHOLE!
NO TOUCHING, BUSTER!
BLAIR, TAKE A BREAK!

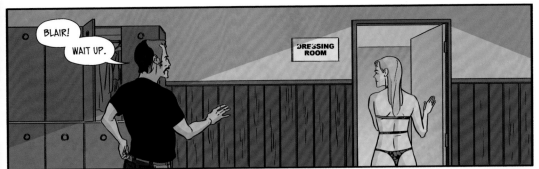

BLAIR!

WAIT UP.

DRESSING ROOM

HERE. COUPLE SAWBUCKS FOR THE SQUEEZE.

I DON'T WANT IT, DALLAS.

DO WHAT YOU WANT, BLAIR, BUT DON'T GIVE IT AWAY FOR FREE.

THEY AREN'T SUPPOSED TO TOUCH.

IT'S PART OF THE JOB.

IT IS NOT!

IF YOU CAN'T GET INTO THE SPIRIT OF THIS GIG, YOU WON'T BE IN IT LONG. YOU PLAY IT RIGHT, YOU'LL BE MAKING A C-NOTE AN HOUR.

NO MEANS NO.

DOES IT?

I HEARD YOUR FRIEND LANA WAS ASKING QUESTIONS AROUND TOWN. ABOUT THINGS THAT ARE NONE OF HER BUSINESS.

SEE HOW EASY THAT WAS?

"JUST WATCHING YOUR BACK, BLAIR. YOU'RE MY BEST GIRL."

THAT WAS INTERESTING.

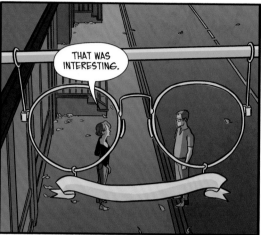

YOU SURE ABOUT WHAT YOU TOLD ME?

IT'S IN THE POLICE NOTES. THE COPS HAULED BETTY GALLAGHER IN TWICE. THEY SUSPECTED SHE WAS RUNNING BOOKMAKING CASH TO THE CITY FOR BYRNE.

YOU'RE BLEEDING. SHOULDN'T YOU REPORT THE ASSAULT TO THE COPS?

NOT YET.

THEY COULD HAVE KILLED YOU.

THEY ALSO MADE A MISTAKE. BY COMING AFTER ME, THEY TIPPED THEIR HAND. MARTY BYRNE IS STILL ALIVE.

YOU'RE NOT GOING TO DO ANYTHING STUPID, ARE YOU?

NO, LETTING YOU KISS ME WAS STUPID ENOUGH.

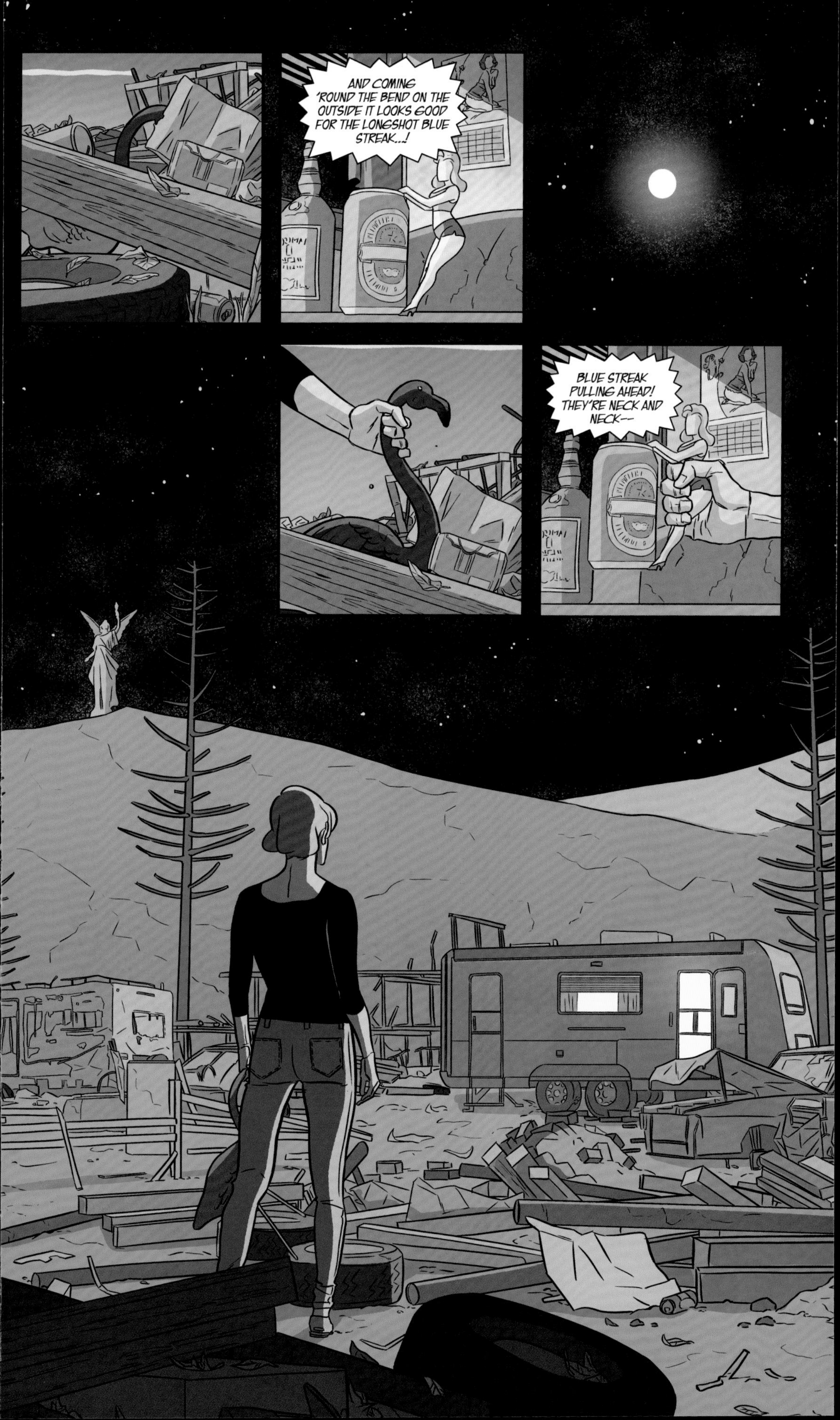
AND COMING 'ROUND THE BEND ON THE OUTSIDE IT LOOKS GOOD FOR THE LONGSHOT BLUE STREAK...!
BLUE STREAK PULLING AHEAD! THEY'RE NECK AND NECK--

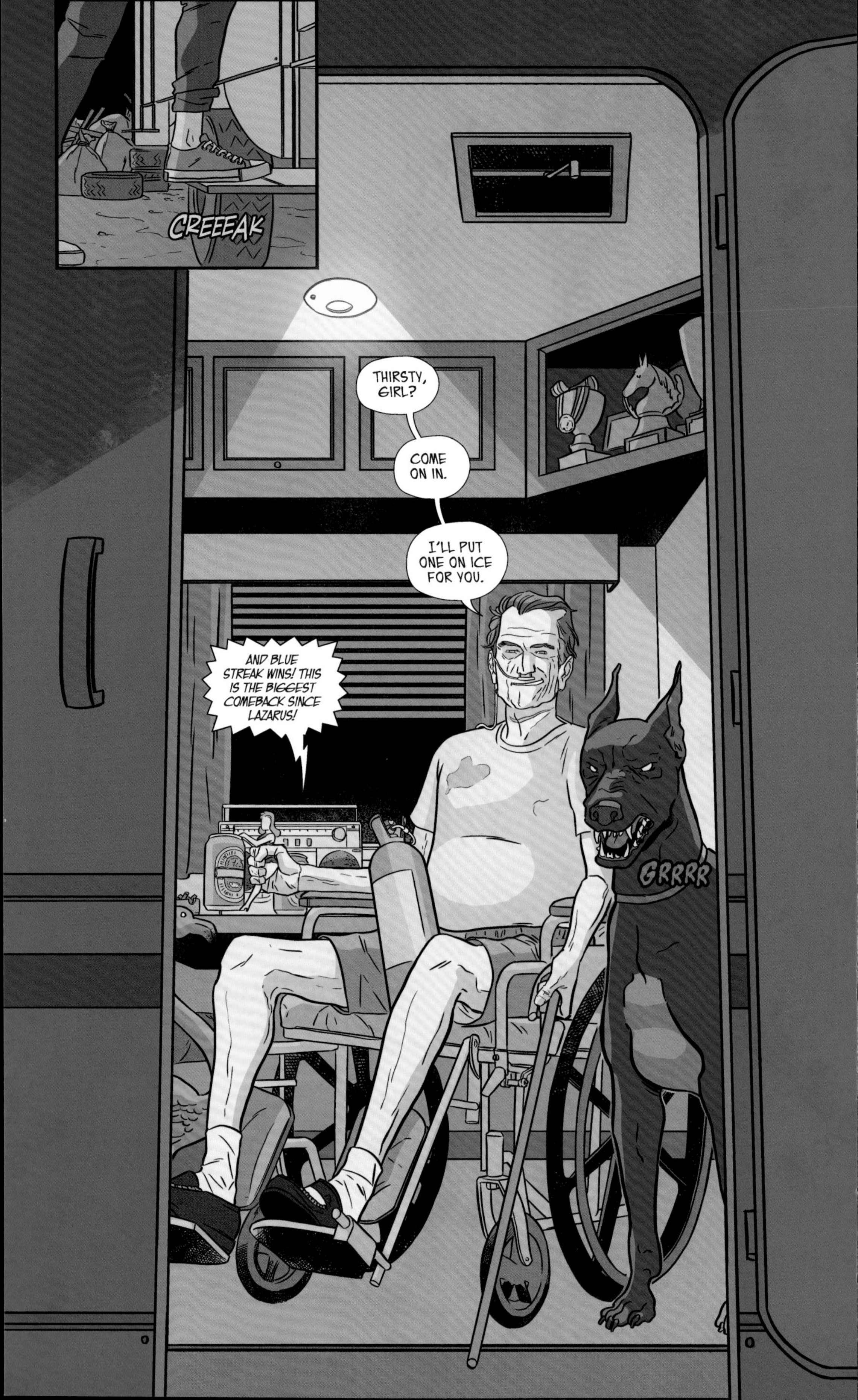
CREEEAK
THIRSTY, GIRL?
COME ON IN.
I'LL PUT ONE ON ICE FOR YOU.
AND BLUE STREAK WINS! THIS IS THE BIGGEST COMEBACK SINCE LAZARUS!
GRRRR

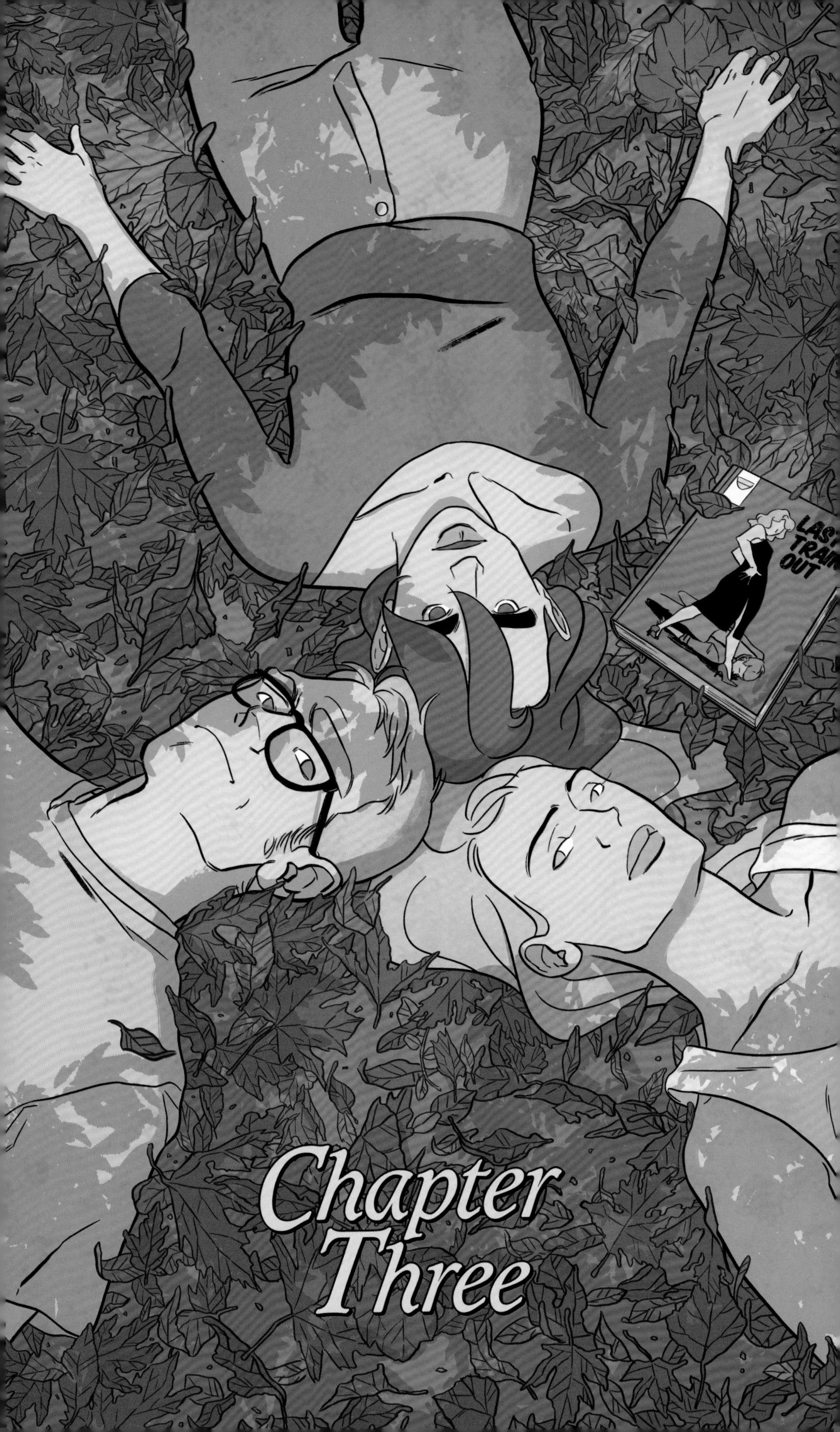
Chapter
Three

> *One of the keys*
>
> *to happiness*
>
> *is a bad memory.*

~RITA MAE BROWN

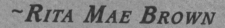

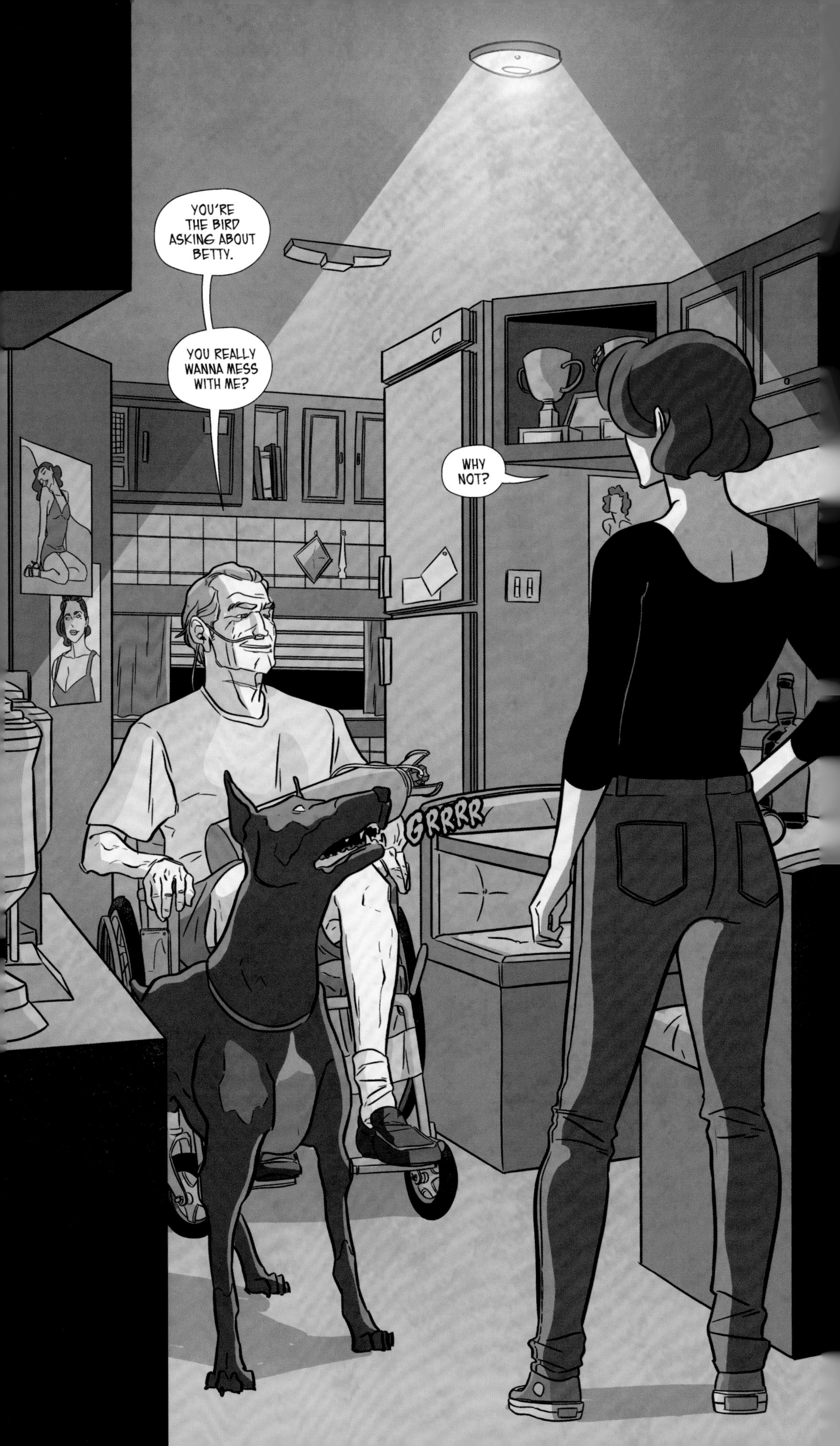
YOU'RE THE BIRD ASKING ABOUT BETTY.
YOU REALLY WANNA MESS WITH ME?
WHY NOT?
GRRRR

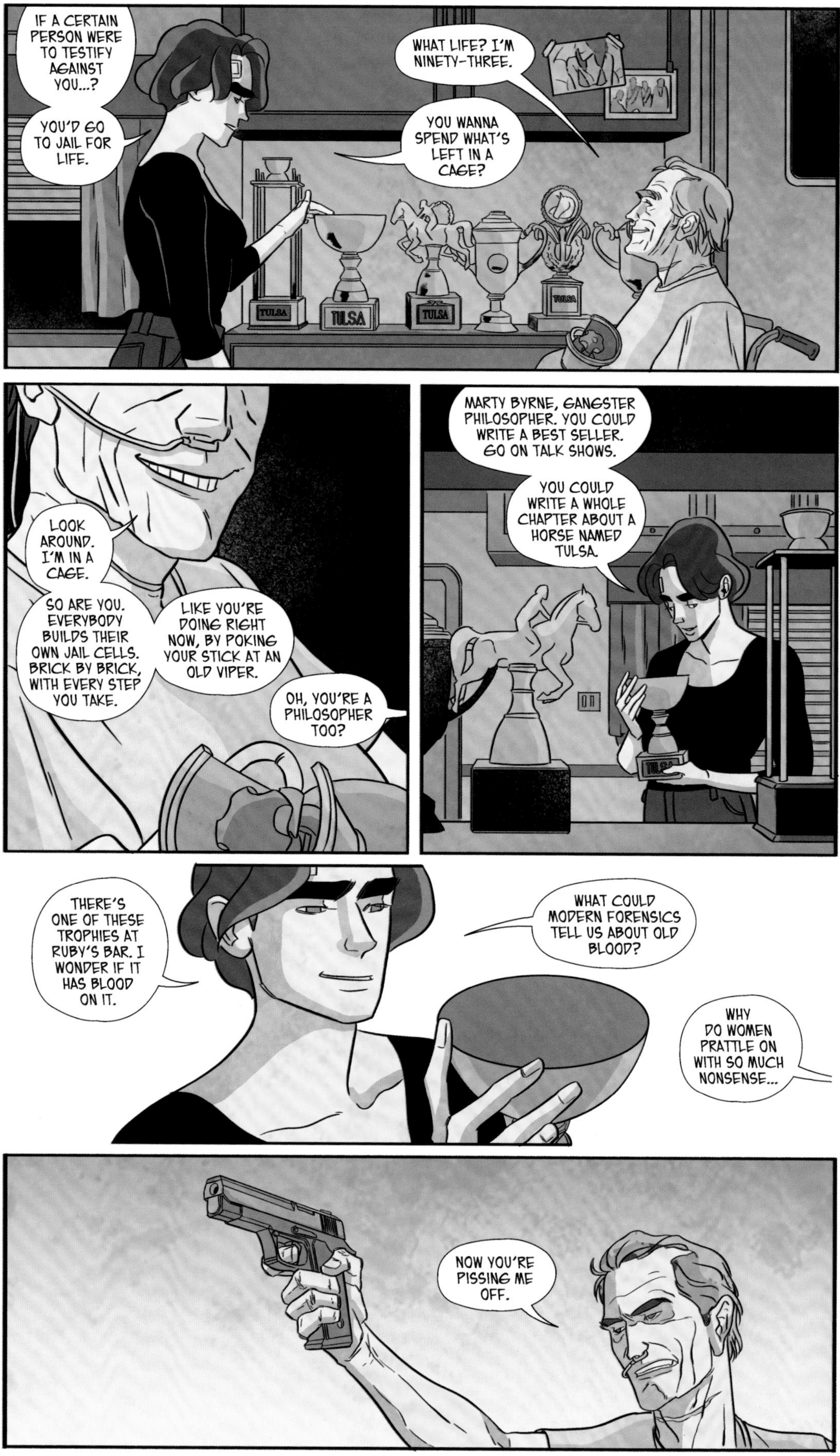
IF A CERTAIN PERSON WERE TO TESTIFY AGAINST YOU...?
YOU'D GO TO JAIL FOR LIFE.
WHAT LIFE? I'M NINETY-THREE.
YOU WANNA SPEND WHAT'S LEFT IN A CAGE?
TULSA
TULSA
TULSA
TULSA
LOOK AROUND. I'M IN A CAGE.
SO ARE YOU. EVERYBODY BUILDS THEIR OWN JAIL CELLS. BRICK BY BRICK, WITH EVERY STEP YOU TAKE.
LIKE YOU'RE DOING RIGHT NOW, BY POKING YOUR STICK AT AN OLD VIPER.
OH, YOU'RE A PHILOSOPHER TOO?
MARTY BYRNE, GANGSTER PHILOSOPHER. YOU COULD WRITE A BEST SELLER. GO ON TALK SHOWS.
YOU COULD WRITE A WHOLE CHAPTER ABOUT A HORSE NAMED TULSA.
THERE'S ONE OF THESE TROPHIES AT RUBY'S BAR. I WONDER IF IT HAS BLOOD ON IT.
WHAT COULD MODERN FORENSICS TELL US ABOUT OLD BLOOD?
WHY DO WOMEN PRATTLE ON WITH SO MUCH NONSENSE...
NOW YOU'RE PISSING ME OFF.

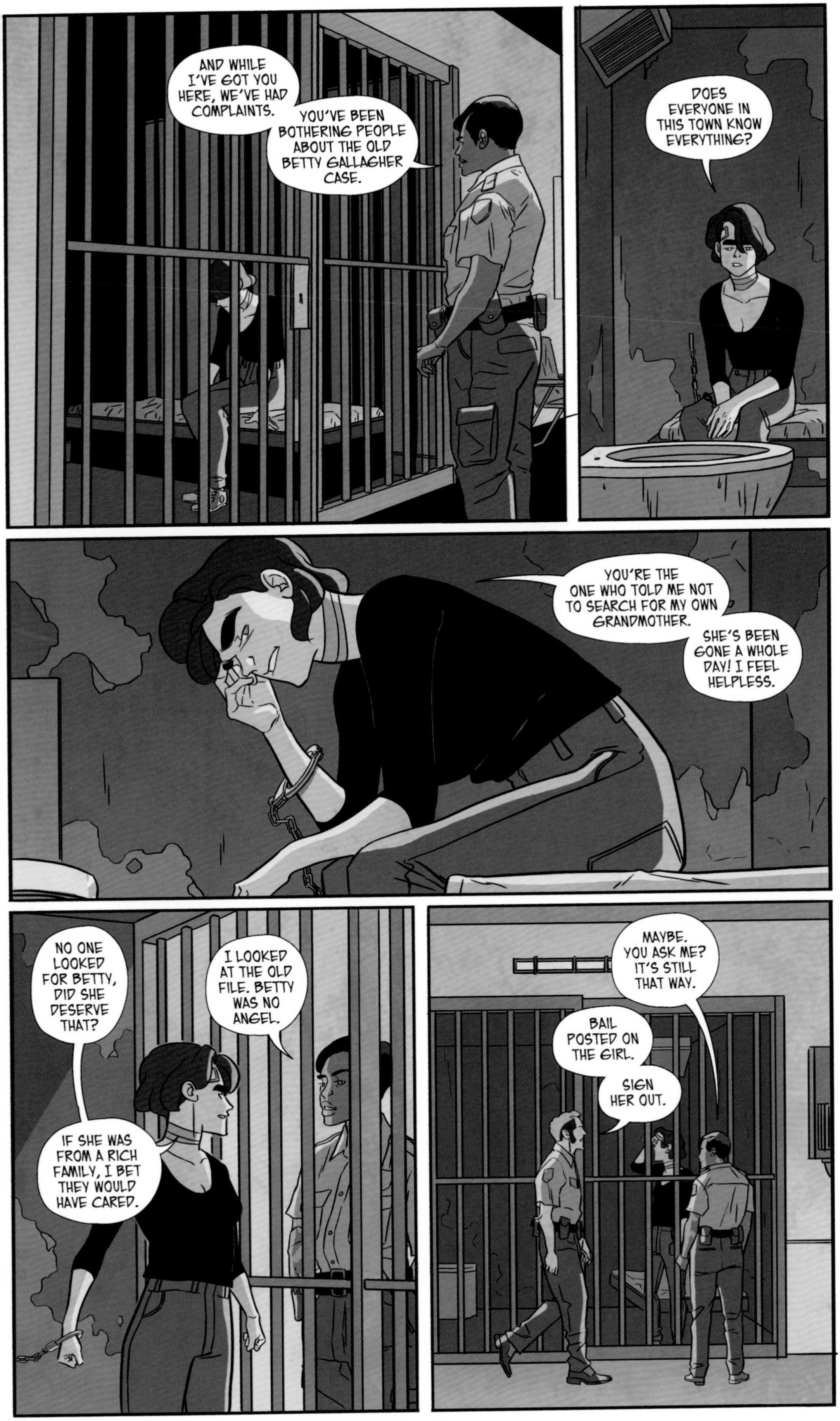
AND WHILE I'VE GOT YOU HERE, WE'VE HAD COMPLAINTS.
YOU'VE BEEN BOTHERING PEOPLE ABOUT THE OLD BETTY GALLAGHER CASE.
DOES EVERYONE IN THIS TOWN KNOW EVERYTHING?
YOU'RE THE ONE WHO TOLD ME NOT TO SEARCH FOR MY OWN GRANDMOTHER.
SHE'S BEEN GONE A WHOLE DAY! I FEEL HELPLESS.
NO ONE LOOKED FOR BETTY, DID SHE DESERVE THAT?
I LOOKED AT THE OLD FILE. BETTY WAS NO ANGEL.
IF SHE WAS FROM A RICH FAMILY, I BET THEY WOULD HAVE CARED.
MAYBE. YOU ASK ME? IT'S STILL THAT WAY.
BAIL POSTED ON THE GIRL.
SIGN HER OUT.

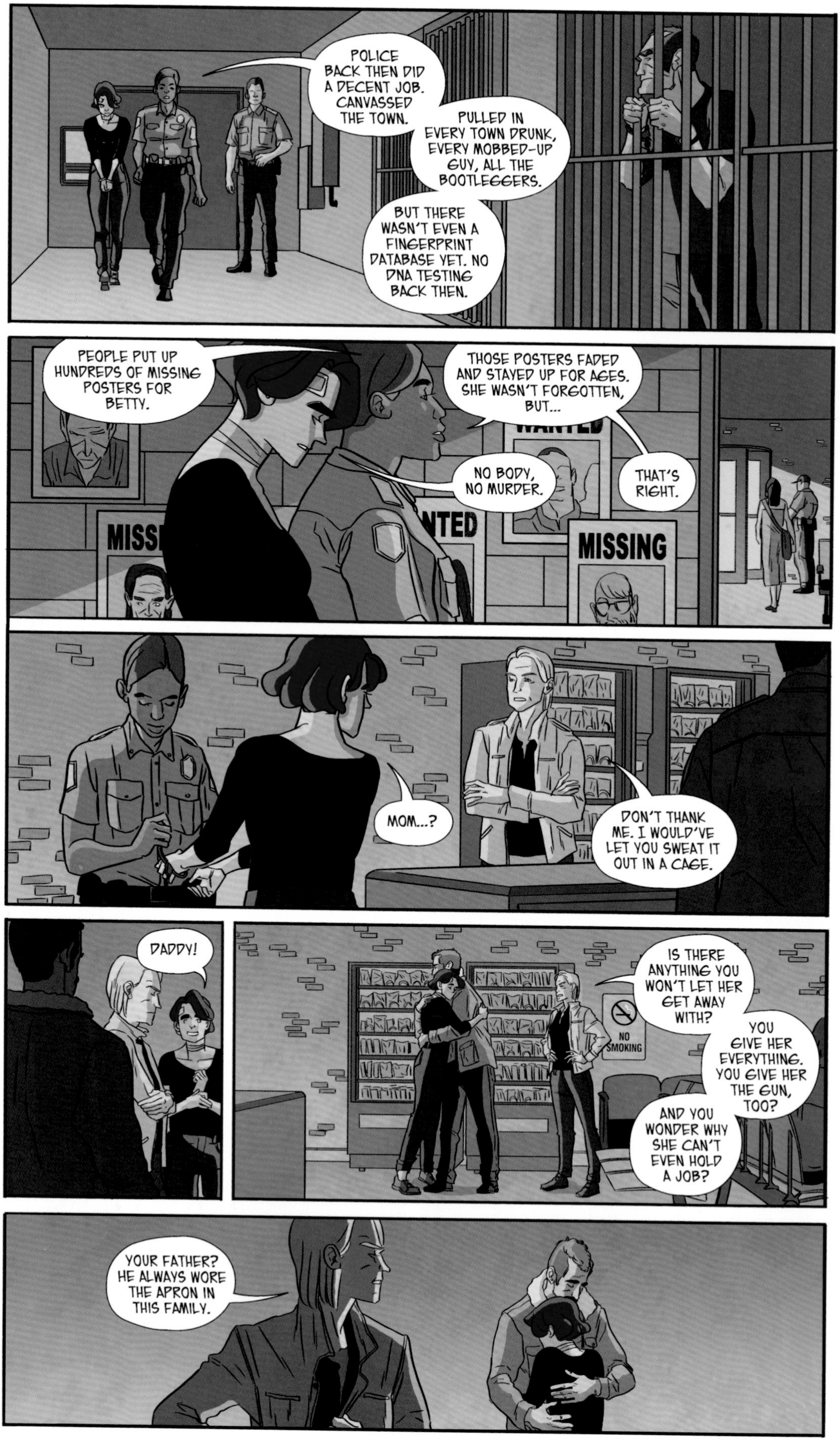
POLICE BACK THEN DID A DECENT JOB. CANVASSED THE TOWN.
PULLED IN EVERY TOWN DRUNK, EVERY MOBBED-UP GUY, ALL THE BOOTLEGGERS.
BUT THERE WASN'T EVEN A FINGERPRINT DATABASE YET. NO DNA TESTING BACK THEN.
PEOPLE PUT UP HUNDREDS OF MISSING POSTERS FOR BETTY.
THOSE POSTERS FADED AND STAYED UP FOR AGES. SHE WASN'T FORGOTTEN, BUT...
NO BODY, NO MURDER.
THAT'S RIGHT.
MISSING
MISSING
MOM...?
DON'T THANK ME. I WOULD'VE LET YOU SWEAT IT OUT IN A CAGE.
DADDY!
IS THERE ANYTHING YOU WON'T LET HER GET AWAY WITH?
NO SMOKING
YOU GIVE HER EVERYTHING. YOU GIVE HER THE GUN, TOO?
AND YOU WONDER WHY SHE CAN'T EVEN HOLD A JOB?
YOUR FATHER? HE ALWAYS WORE THE APRON IN THIS FAMILY.

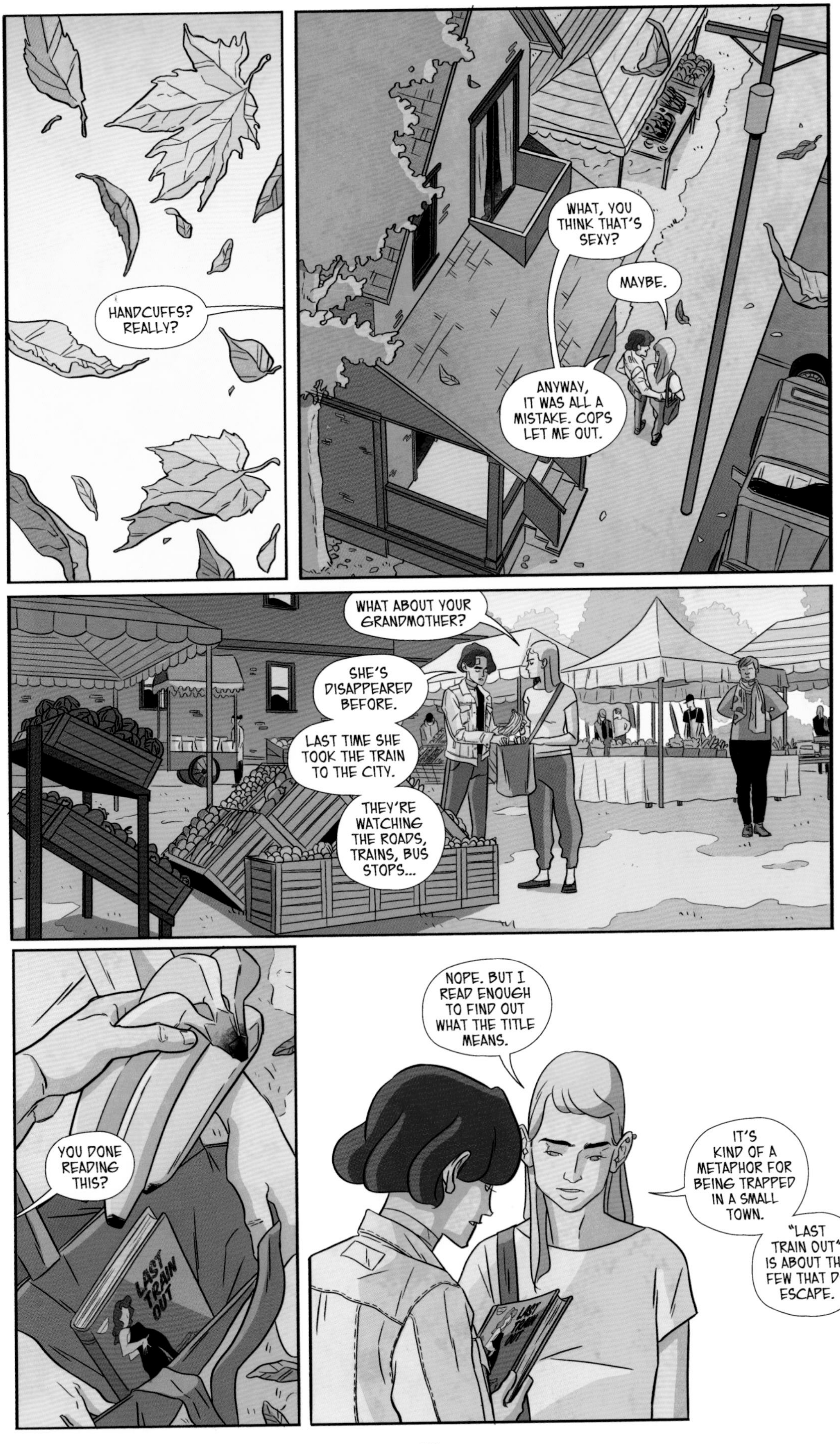
HANDCUFFS? REALLY?
WHAT, YOU THINK THAT'S SEXY?
MAYBE.
ANYWAY, IT WAS ALL A MISTAKE. COPS LET ME OUT.
WHAT ABOUT YOUR GRANDMOTHER?
SHE'S DISAPPEARED BEFORE.
LAST TIME SHE TOOK THE TRAIN TO THE CITY.
THEY'RE WATCHING THE ROADS, TRAINS, BUS STOPS...
YOU DONE READING THIS?
LAST TRAIN OUT
NOPE. BUT I READ ENOUGH TO FIND OUT WHAT THE TITLE MEANS.
IT'S KIND OF A METAPHOR FOR BEING TRAPPED IN A SMALL TOWN.
"LAST TRAIN OUT" IS ABOUT THE FEW THAT DO ESCAPE.

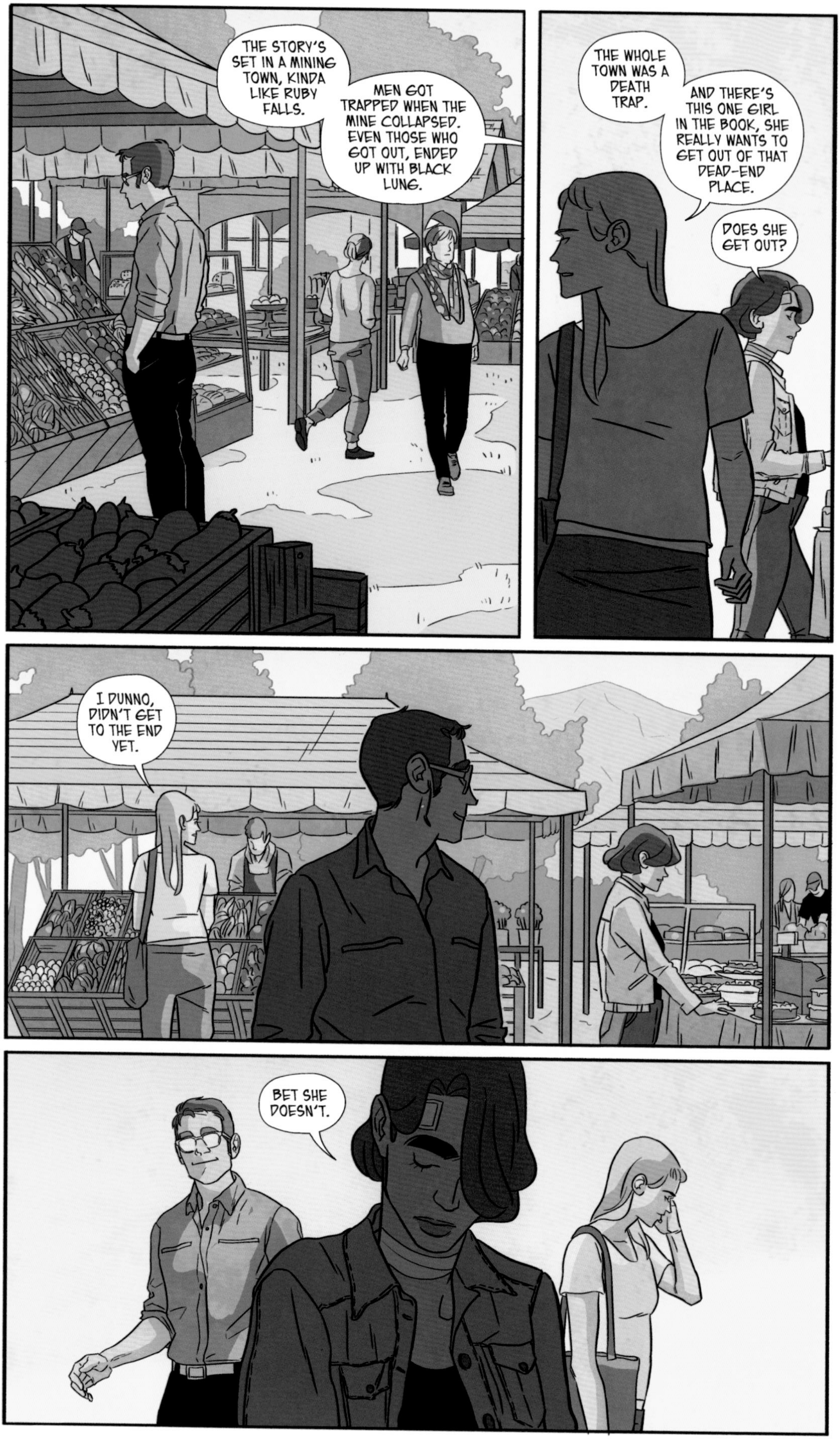
THE STORY'S SET IN A MINING TOWN, KINDA LIKE RUBY FALLS.
MEN GOT TRAPPED WHEN THE MINE COLLAPSED. EVEN THOSE WHO GOT OUT, ENDED UP WITH BLACK LUNG.
THE WHOLE TOWN WAS A DEATH TRAP.
AND THERE'S THIS ONE GIRL IN THE BOOK, SHE REALLY WANTS TO GET OUT OF THAT DEAD-END PLACE.
DOES SHE GET OUT?
I DUNNO, DIDN'T GET TO THE END YET.
BET SHE DOESN'T.

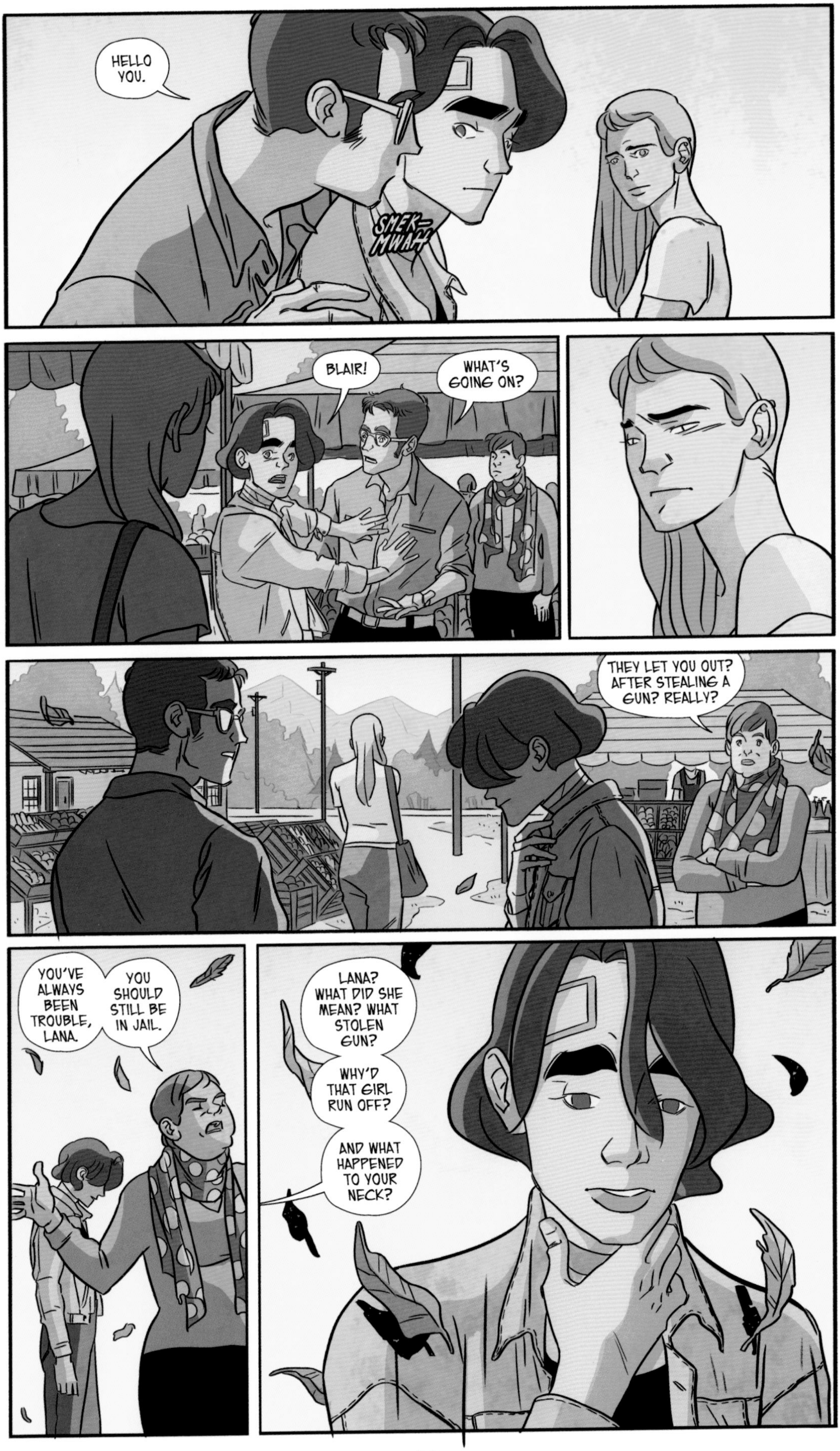
HELLO YOU.
SMEK-MWAH
BLAIR!
WHAT'S GOING ON?
THEY LET YOU OUT? AFTER STEALING A GUN? REALLY?
YOU'VE ALWAYS BEEN TROUBLE, LANA.
YOU SHOULD STILL BE IN JAIL.
LANA? WHAT DID SHE MEAN? WHAT STOLEN GUN?
WHY'D THAT GIRL RUN OFF?
AND WHAT HAPPENED TO YOUR NECK?

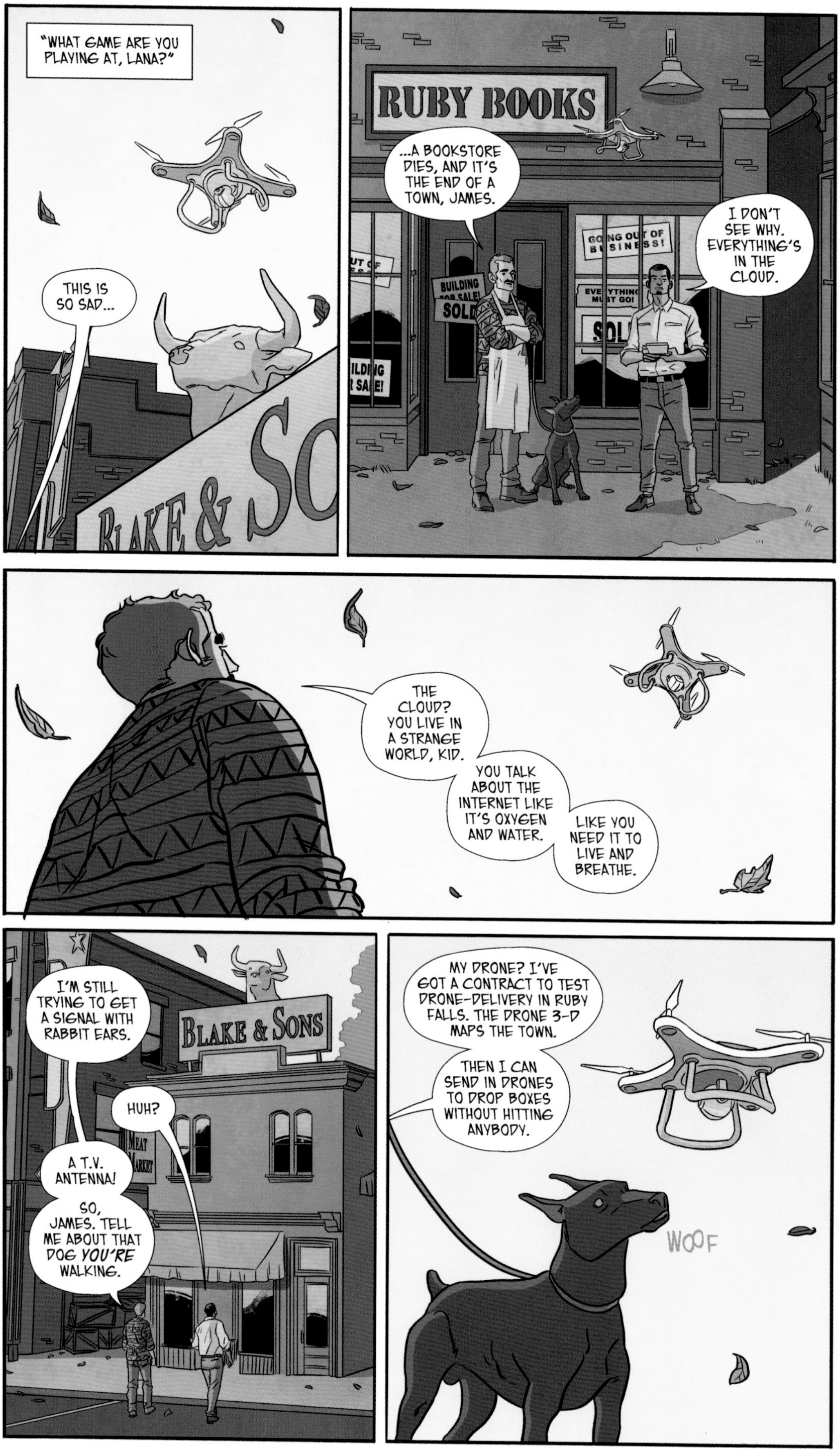
"WHAT GAME ARE YOU PLAYING AT, LANA?"
THIS IS SO SAD...
RUBY BOOKS
...A BOOKSTORE DIES, AND IT'S THE END OF A TOWN, JAMES.
I DON'T SEE WHY. EVERYTHING'S IN THE CLOUD.
THE CLOUD? YOU LIVE IN A STRANGE WORLD, KID.
YOU TALK ABOUT THE INTERNET LIKE IT'S OXYGEN AND WATER.
LIKE YOU NEED IT TO LIVE AND BREATHE.
BLAKE & SONS
I'M STILL TRYING TO GET A SIGNAL WITH RABBIT EARS.
HUH?
A T.V. ANTENNA!
SO, JAMES. TELL ME ABOUT THAT DOG *YOU'RE* WALKING.
MY DRONE? I'VE GOT A CONTRACT TO TEST DRONE-DELIVERY IN RUBY FALLS. THE DRONE 3-D MAPS THE TOWN.
THEN I CAN SEND IN DRONES TO DROP BOXES WITHOUT HITTING ANYBODY.
WOOF

ONCE I'VE ACQUIRED ALL THE GPS DATA, I'LL TOSS UP A VIRTUAL FENCE AND CAPTURE CONSUMERS.

THEN I'LL STALK THEM, FOR SALES.

I DON'T KNOW WHAT YOU JUST SAID, BUT IT SURE SOUNDS LIKE A FOX CASING A HEN HOUSE.

BUT I DO WANT YOUR IDEAS ON HOW TO GROW MY BUSINESS.

I'M WORRIED ABOUT MY DAUGHTER LANA.

I HEARD SHE WAS ARRESTED. SHE SEEMS A BIT LOST.

SOMETIMES I THINK MAYBE THERE'S SOMETHING BROKEN INSIDE HER. LIKE WE'LL BE BAILING HER OUT FOREVER.

MISSING

HAVE YOU S THIS WOMA

I NEED TO PUT MORE ON THE TABLE.

I SEE. WELL, BLAKE, IF YOU WON'T EVEN CONSIDER AN ONLINE MARKET FOR YOUR MEAT...YOU'LL GO THE WAY OF THE BOOKSTORE.

FREE RANGE, ORGANIC, RAISED WITH LOVE? I COULD BRAND THE SHIT OUTTA YOUR MEAT.

IS THIS ONE OF THOSE "CHANGE OR DIE" SITUATIONS?

MIGHT BE, OLD MAN.

69

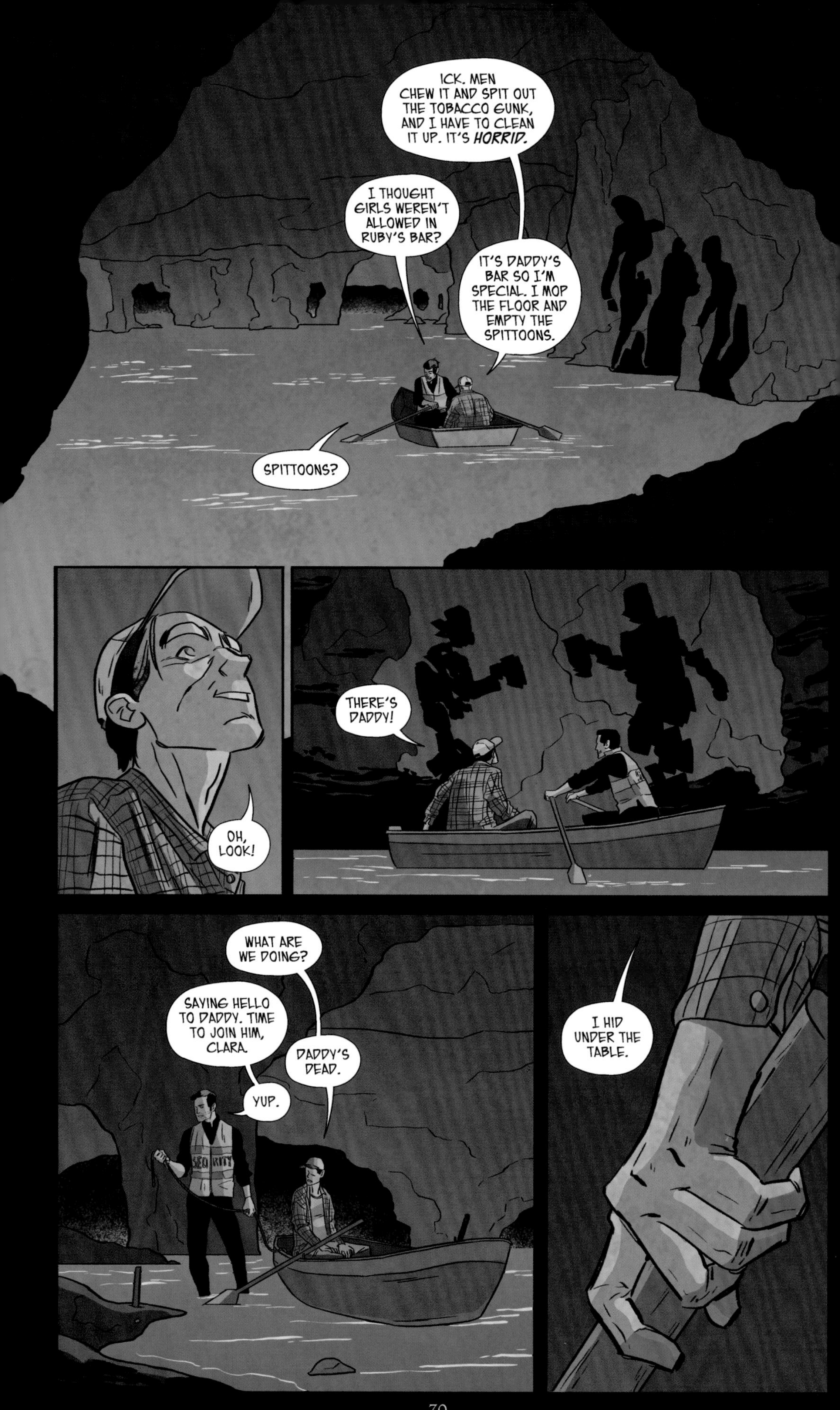
ICK. MEN CHEW IT AND SPIT OUT THE TOBACCO GUNK, AND I HAVE TO CLEAN IT UP. IT'S *HORRID.*
I THOUGHT GIRLS WEREN'T ALLOWED IN RUBY'S BAR?
IT'S DADDY'S BAR SO I'M SPECIAL. I MOP THE FLOOR AND EMPTY THE SPITTOONS.
SPITTOONS?
OH, LOOK!
THERE'S DADDY!
WHAT ARE WE DOING?
SAYING HELLO TO DADDY. TIME TO JOIN HIM, CLARA.
DADDY'S DEAD.
YUP.
I HID UNDER THE TABLE.

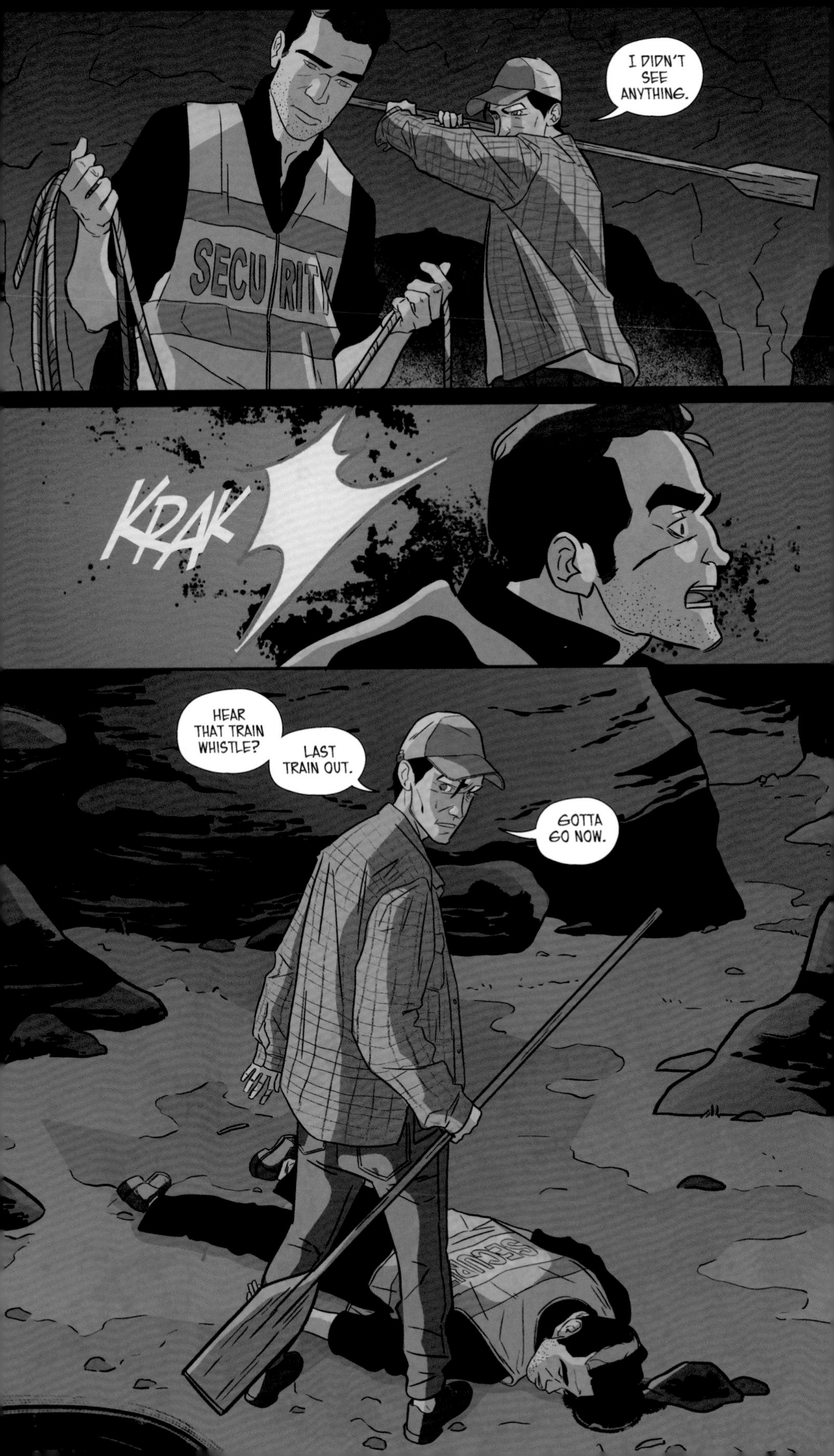

I DIDN'T SEE ANYTHING.
SECURITY
KRAK
HEAR THAT TRAIN WHISTLE?
LAST TRAIN OUT.
GOTTA GO NOW.

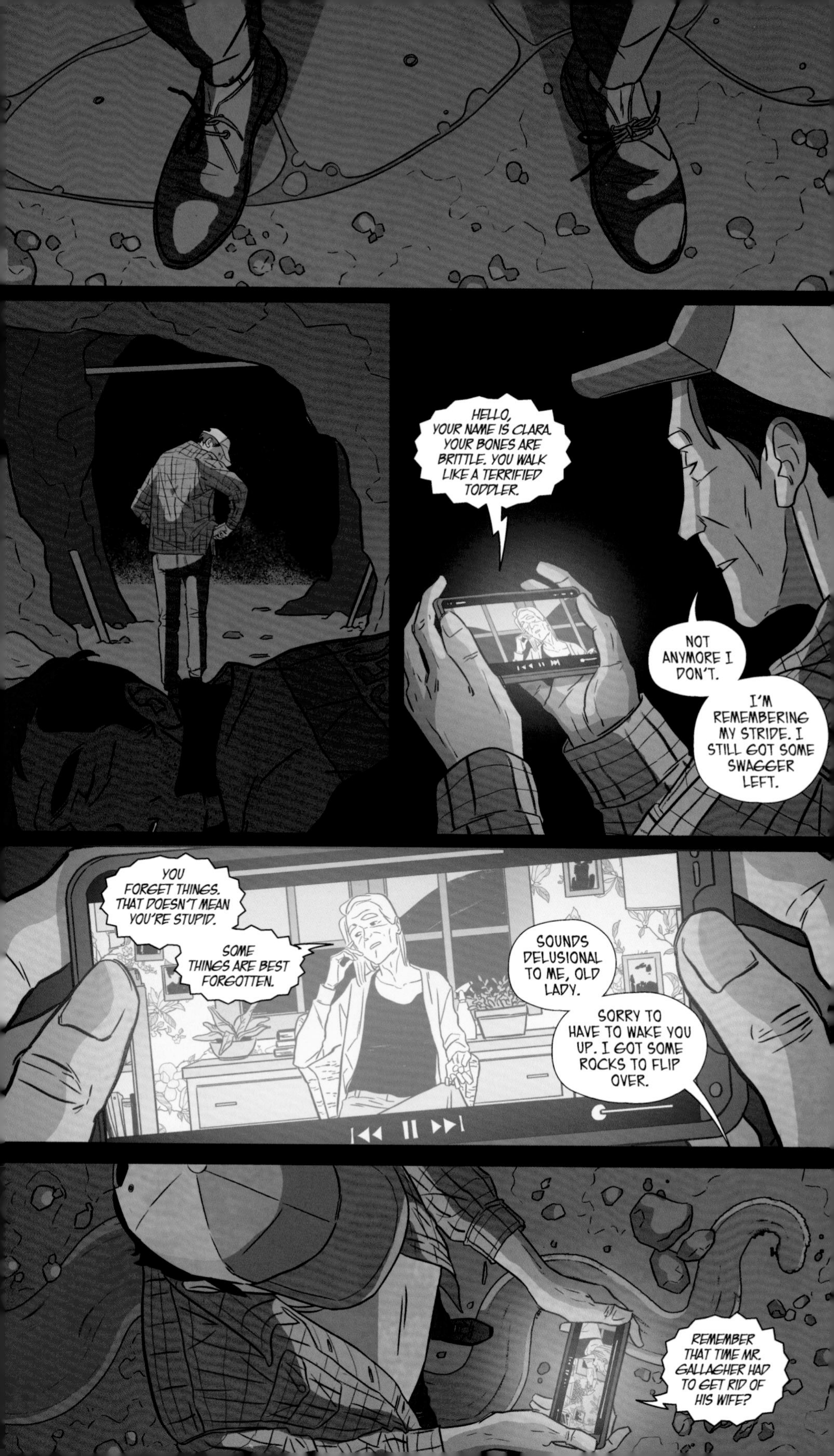
HELLO, YOUR NAME IS CLARA. YOUR BONES ARE BRITTLE. YOU WALK LIKE A TERRIFIED TODDLER.
NOT ANYMORE I DON'T.
I'M REMEMBERING MY STRIDE. I STILL GOT SOME SWAGGER LEFT.
YOU FORGET THINGS. THAT DOESN'T MEAN YOU'RE STUPID.
SOME THINGS ARE BEST FORGOTTEN.
SOUNDS DELUSIONAL TO ME, OLD LADY.
SORRY TO HAVE TO WAKE YOU UP. I GOT SOME ROCKS TO FLIP OVER.
REMEMBER THAT TIME MR. GALLAGHER HAD TO GET RID OF HIS WIFE?

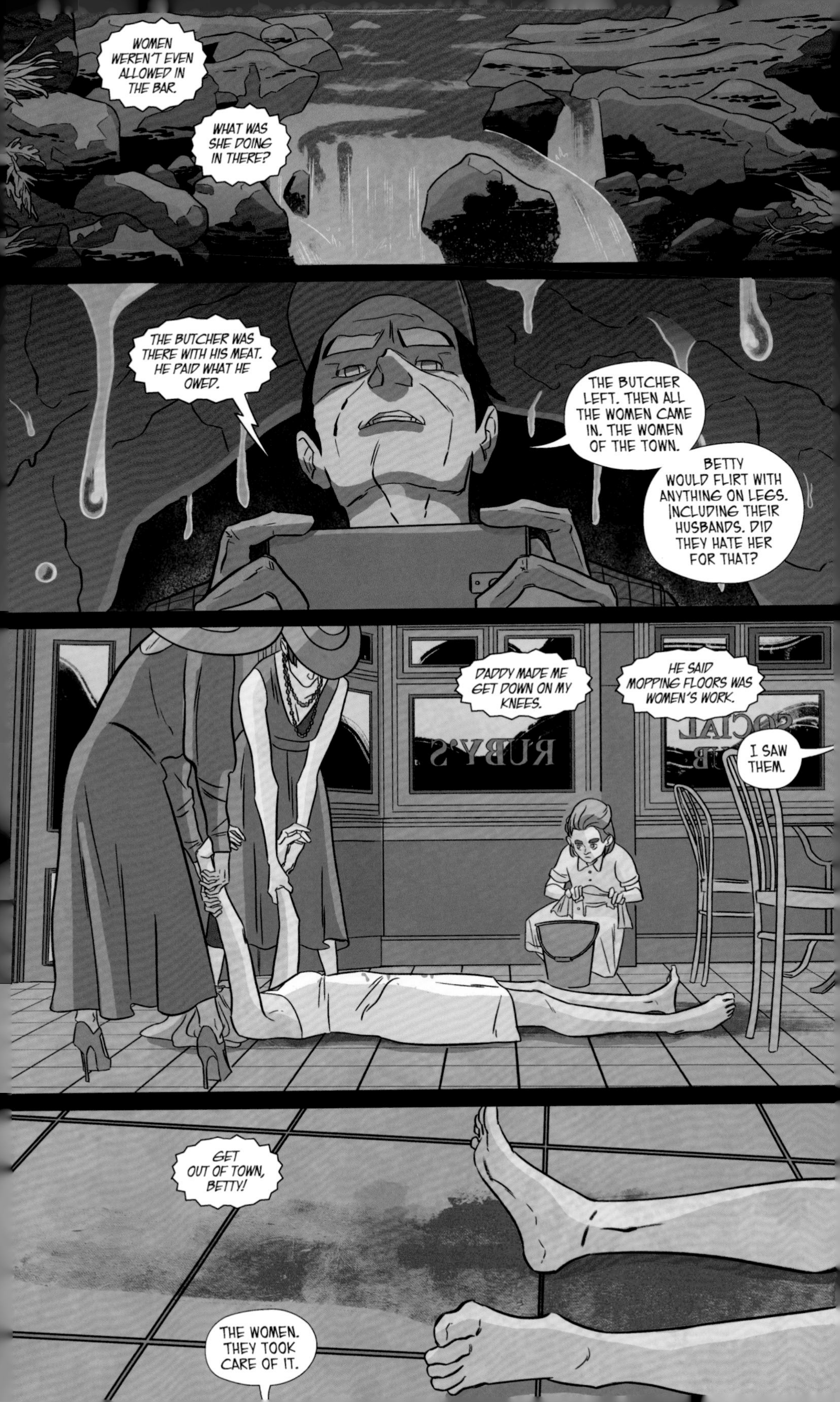
WOMEN WEREN'T EVEN ALLOWED IN THE BAR.
WHAT WAS SHE DOING IN THERE?
THE BUTCHER WAS THERE WITH HIS MEAT. HE PAID WHAT HE OWED.
THE BUTCHER LEFT. THEN ALL THE WOMEN CAME IN. THE WOMEN OF THE TOWN.
BETTY WOULD FLIRT WITH ANYTHING ON LEGS. INCLUDING THEIR HUSBANDS. DID THEY HATE HER FOR THAT?
DADDY MADE ME GET DOWN ON MY KNEES.
HE SAID MOPPING FLOORS WAS WOMEN'S WORK.
I SAW THEM.
GET OUT OF TOWN, BETTY!
THE WOMEN. THEY TOOK CARE OF IT.

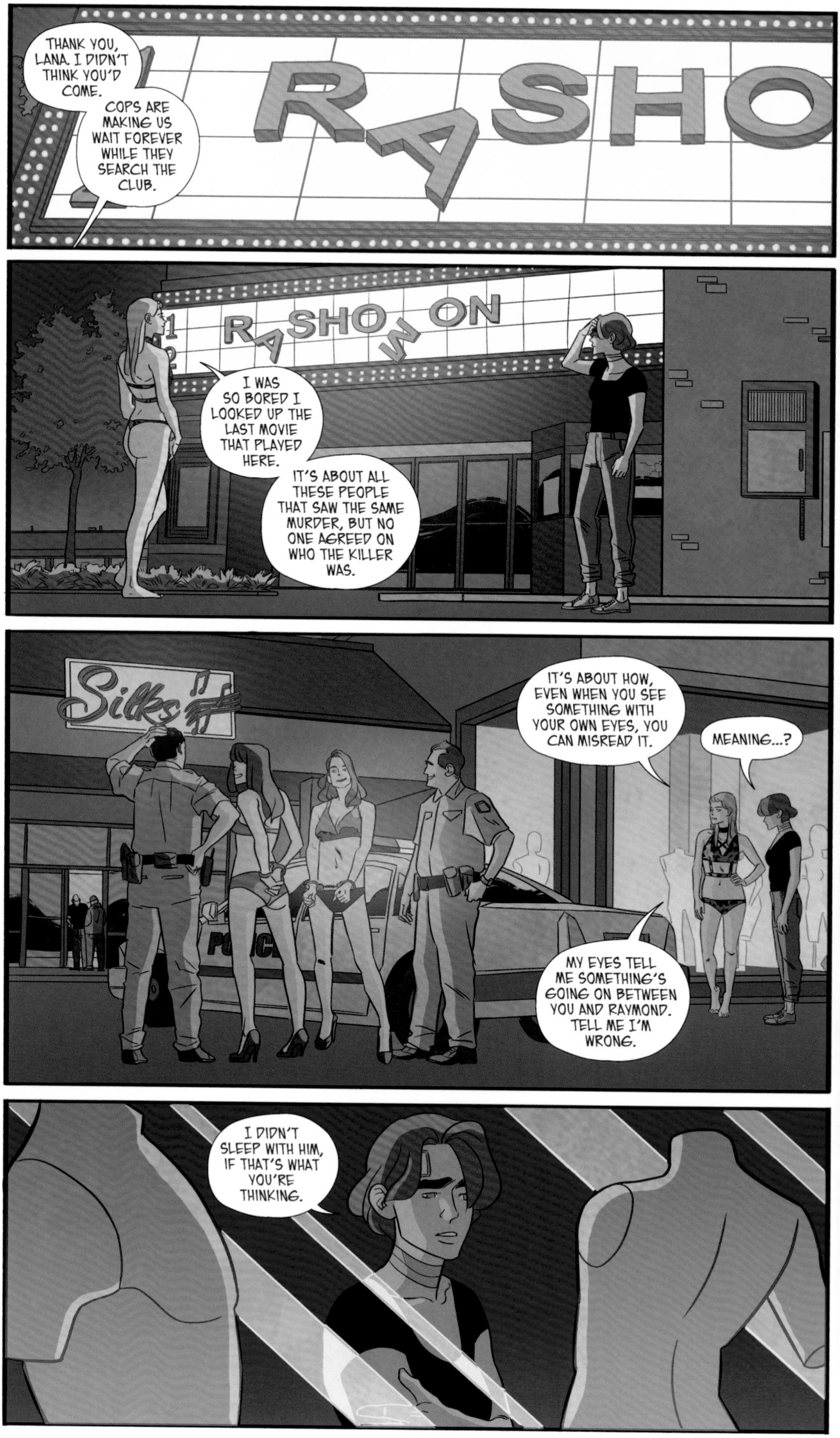
THANK YOU, LANA. I DIDN'T THINK YOU'D COME.
COPS ARE MAKING US WAIT FOREVER WHILE THEY SEARCH THE CLUB.
RASHO
RASHOWON
I WAS SO BORED I LOOKED UP THE LAST MOVIE THAT PLAYED HERE.
IT'S ABOUT ALL THESE PEOPLE THAT SAW THE SAME MURDER, BUT NO ONE AGREED ON WHO THE KILLER WAS.
Silks
POLICE
IT'S ABOUT HOW, EVEN WHEN YOU SEE SOMETHING WITH YOUR OWN EYES, YOU CAN MISREAD IT.
MEANING...?
MY EYES TELL ME SOMETHING'S GOING ON BETWEEN YOU AND RAYMOND. TELL ME I'M WRONG.
I DIDN'T SLEEP WITH HIM, IF THAT'S WHAT YOU'RE THINKING.

I FLIRTED WITH HIM, THAT'S ALL.

HE HAS ACCESS TO THE MUNICIPAL POLICE ARCHIVES. SO YEAH, I USED HIM.

DON'T WORRY, HE WANTS NOTHING MORE TO DO WITH ME.

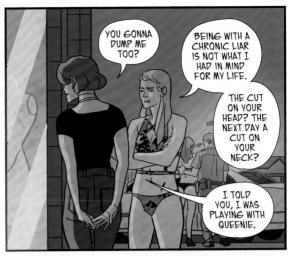

YOU GONNA DUMP ME TOO?

BEING WITH A CHRONIC LIAR IS NOT WHAT I HAD IN MIND FOR MY LIFE.

THE CUT ON YOUR HEAD? THE NEXT DAY A CUT ON YOUR NECK?

I TOLD YOU, I WAS PLAYING WITH QUEENIE.

YOU HAVE A "TELL" AS THEY SAY IN POKER. YOU TURN YOUR HEAD AWAY WHEN YOU LIE.

BLAIR?

COPS SHUT US DOWN FOR THE NIGHT. YOU CAN GO HOME.

AND THE OTHER GIRLS?!

COPS WON'T CHARGE THEM, LONG AS THEY LEAVE TOWN. I GAVE THEM TRAIN FARE TO THE CITY.

SO THAT'S HOW IT WORKS, HUH? THE CLIENTS DON'T GET BUSTED? YOU DON'T GET BUSTED?

BUT THE GIRLS GET THROWN OUT OF TOWN?

YOU WANT THIS JOB OR NOT?

FORGET THAT JERK. GET YOUR STUFF.

I'LL TELL YOU EVERYTHING.

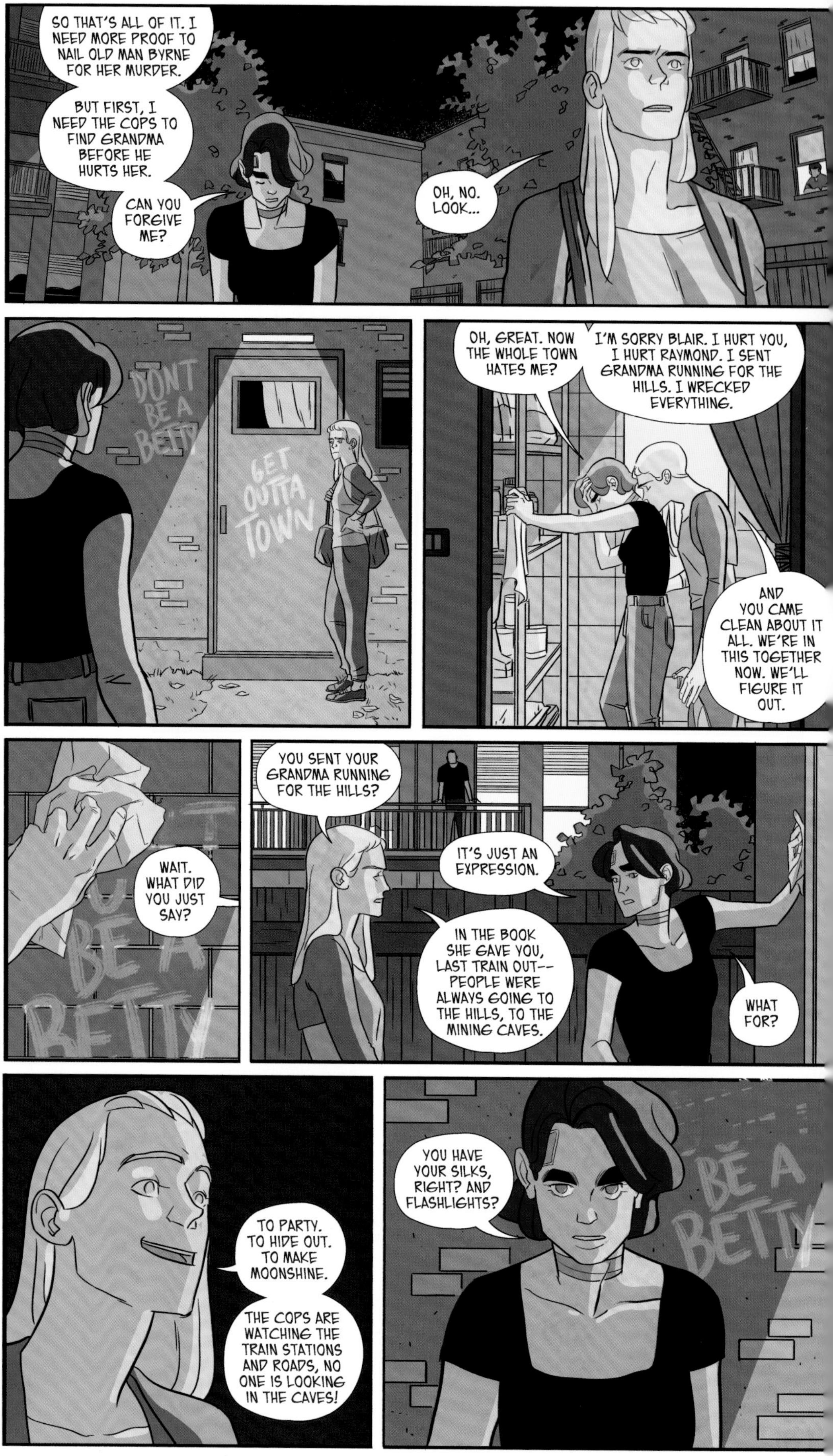
SO THAT'S ALL OF IT. I NEED MORE PROOF TO NAIL OLD MAN BYRNE FOR HER MURDER.
BUT FIRST, I NEED THE COPS TO FIND GRANDMA BEFORE HE HURTS HER.
CAN YOU FORGIVE ME?
OH, NO. LOOK...
DON'T BE A BETTY
GET OUTTA TOWN
OH, GREAT. NOW THE WHOLE TOWN HATES ME?
I'M SORRY BLAIR. I HURT YOU, I HURT RAYMOND. I SENT GRANDMA RUNNING FOR THE HILLS. I WRECKED EVERYTHING.
AND YOU CAME CLEAN ABOUT IT ALL. WE'RE IN THIS TOGETHER NOW. WE'LL FIGURE IT OUT.
WAIT. WHAT DID YOU JUST SAY?
BE A BETTY
YOU SENT YOUR GRANDMA RUNNING FOR THE HILLS?
IT'S JUST AN EXPRESSION.
IN THE BOOK SHE GAVE YOU, LAST TRAIN OUT-- PEOPLE WERE ALWAYS GOING TO THE HILLS, TO THE MINING CAVES.
WHAT FOR?
TO PARTY. TO HIDE OUT. TO MAKE MOONSHINE.
THE COPS ARE WATCHING THE TRAIN STATIONS AND ROADS, NO ONE IS LOOKING IN THE CAVES!
YOU HAVE YOUR SILKS, RIGHT? AND FLASHLIGHTS?
BE A BETTY

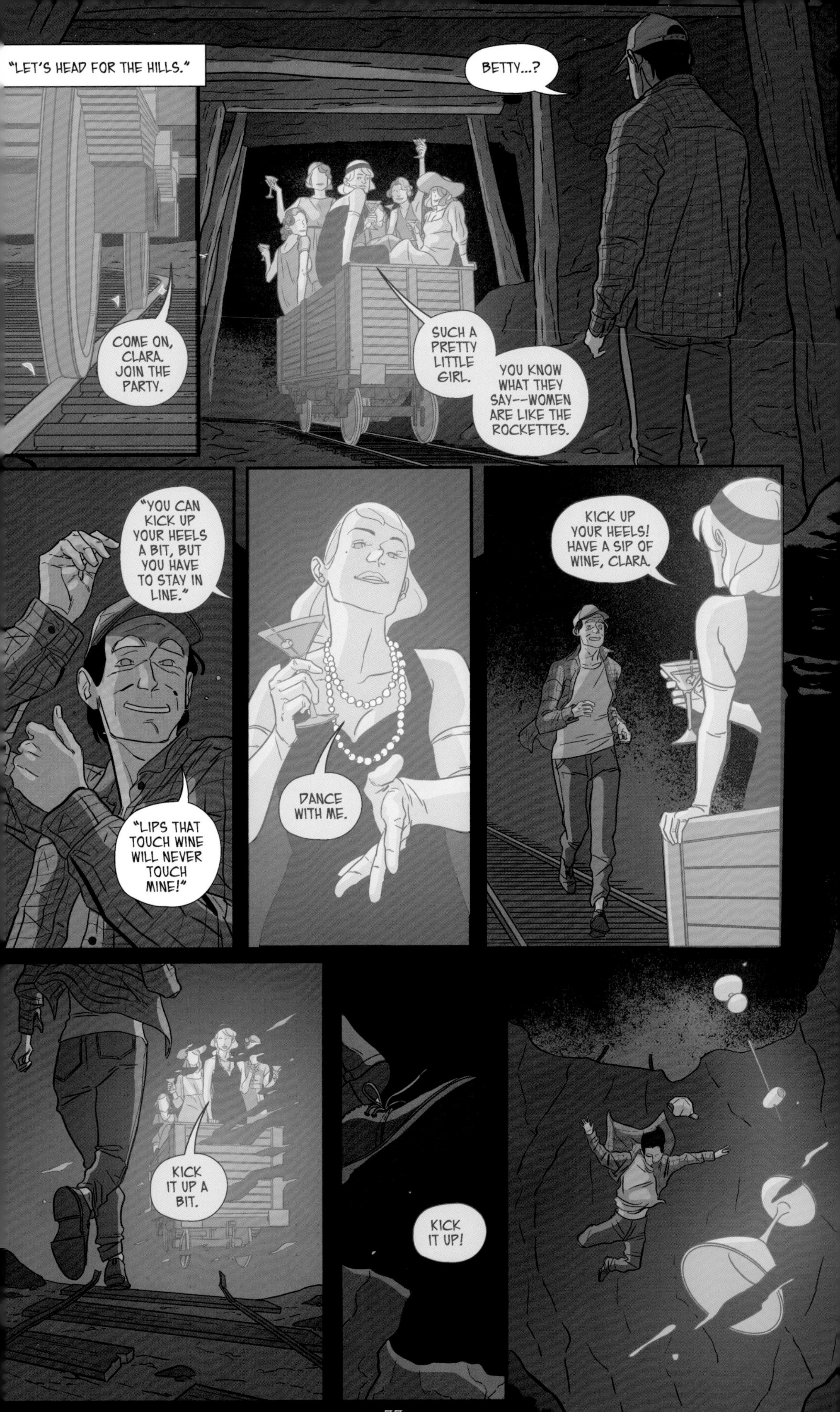
"LET'S HEAD FOR THE HILLS."
BETTY...?
COME ON, CLARA. JOIN THE PARTY.
SUCH A PRETTY LITTLE GIRL.
YOU KNOW WHAT THEY SAY--WOMEN ARE LIKE THE ROCKETTES.
"YOU CAN KICK UP YOUR HEELS A BIT, BUT YOU HAVE TO STAY IN LINE."
"LIPS THAT TOUCH WINE WILL NEVER TOUCH MINE!"
DANCE WITH ME.
KICK UP YOUR HEELS! HAVE A SIP OF WINE, CLARA.
KICK IT UP A BIT.
KICK IT UP!

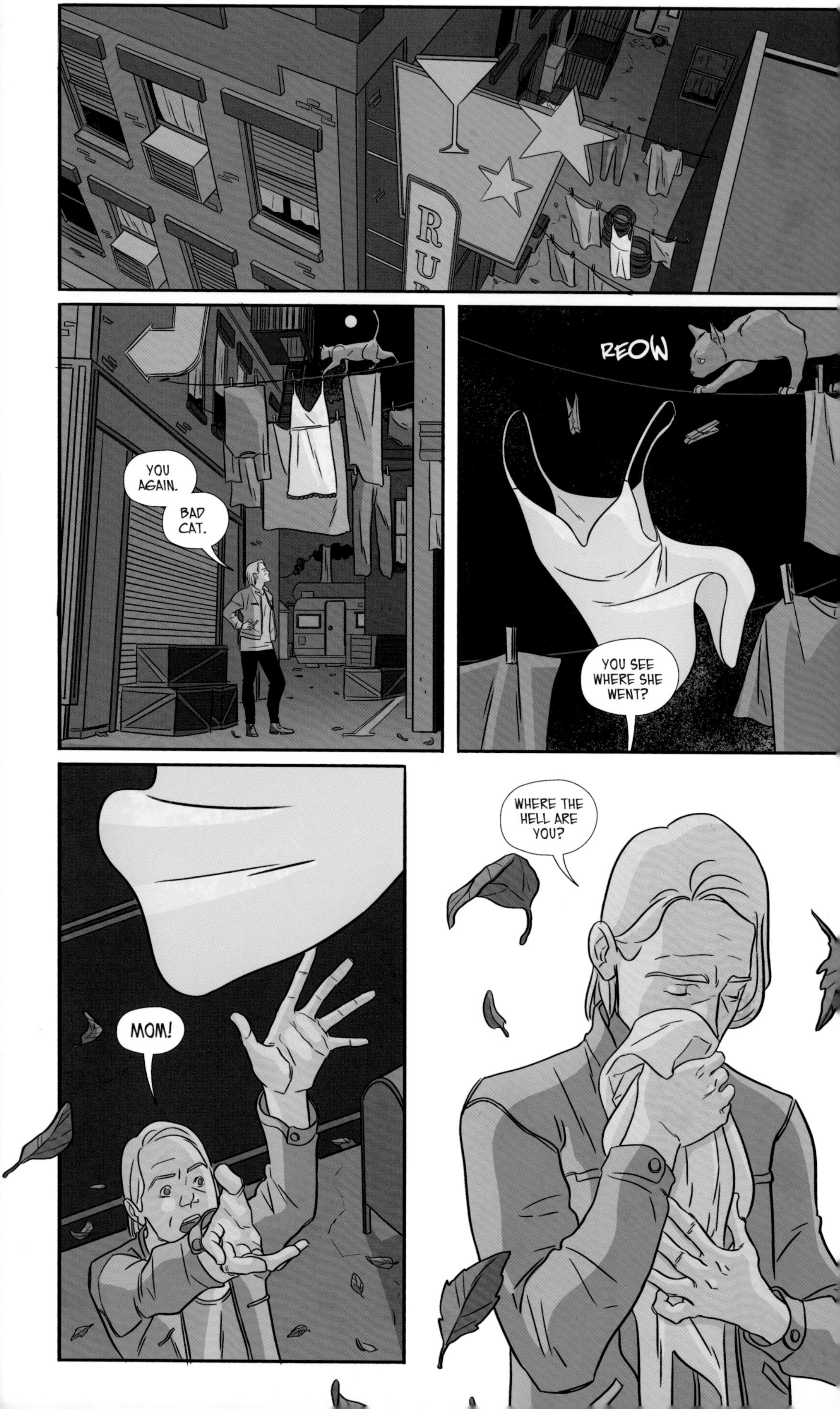

YOU AGAIN.
BAD CAT.
REOW
YOU SEE WHERE SHE WENT?
MOM!
WHERE THE HELL ARE YOU?

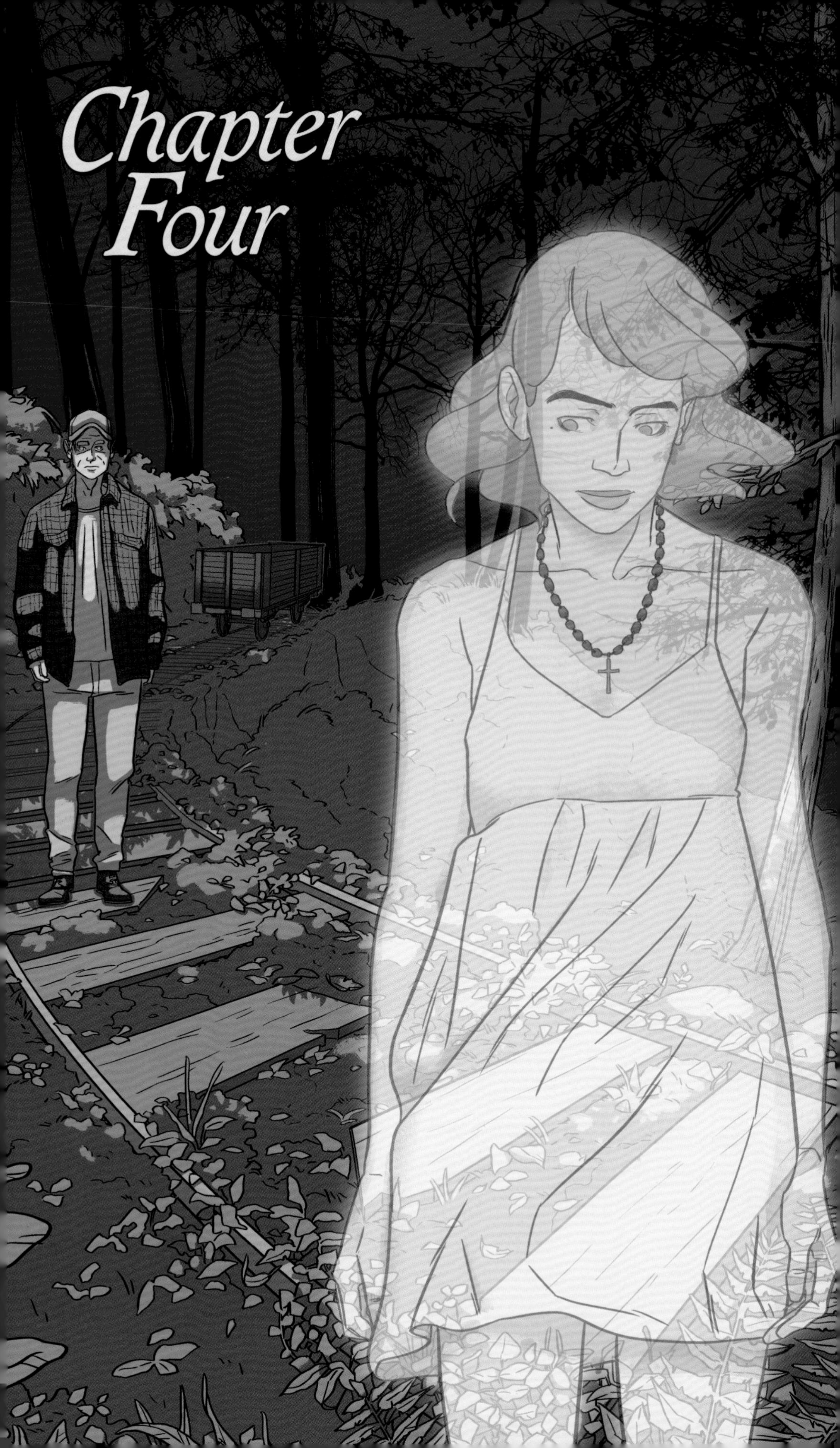
Chapter Four

❝ *There must be eyes upon the street, eyes belonging to those we might call the natural proprietors of the street.* **❞**

~HISTORIAN
JANE JACOBS

❝ *When the legend becomes fact, print the legend.* **❞**

~THE MAN WHO SHOT
LIBERTY VALANCE

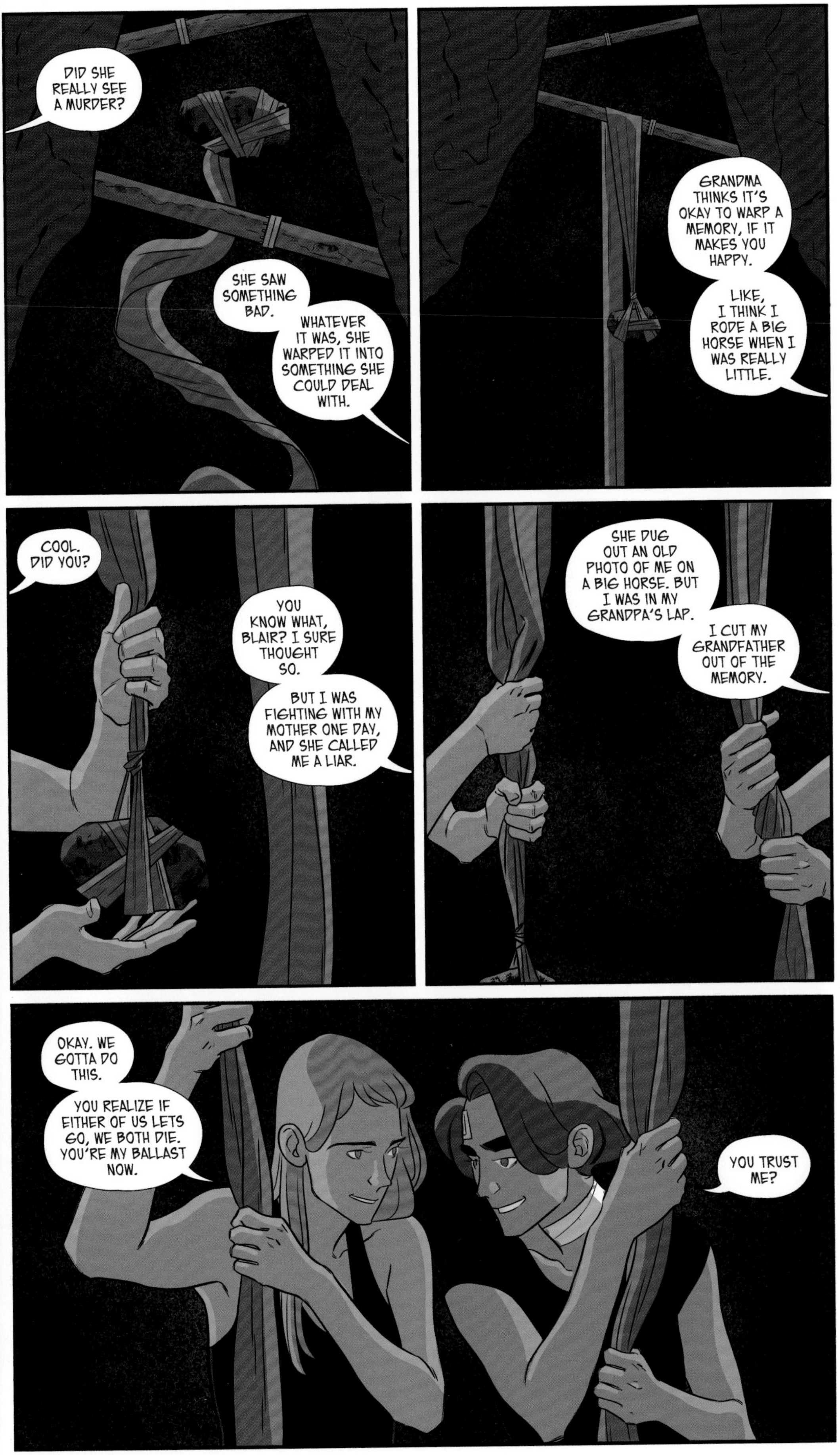
DID SHE REALLY SEE A MURDER?
SHE SAW SOMETHING BAD.
WHATEVER IT WAS, SHE WARPED IT INTO SOMETHING SHE COULD DEAL WITH.
GRANDMA THINKS IT'S OKAY TO WARP A MEMORY, IF IT MAKES YOU HAPPY.
LIKE, I THINK I RODE A BIG HORSE WHEN I WAS REALLY LITTLE.
COOL. DID YOU?
YOU KNOW WHAT, BLAIR? I SURE THOUGHT SO.
BUT I WAS FIGHTING WITH MY MOTHER ONE DAY, AND SHE CALLED ME A LIAR.
SHE DUG OUT AN OLD PHOTO OF ME ON A BIG HORSE. BUT I WAS IN MY GRANDPA'S LAP.
I CUT MY GRANDFATHER OUT OF THE MEMORY.
OKAY. WE GOTTA DO THIS.
YOU REALIZE IF EITHER OF US LETS GO, WE BOTH DIE. YOU'RE MY BALLAST NOW.
YOU TRUST ME?

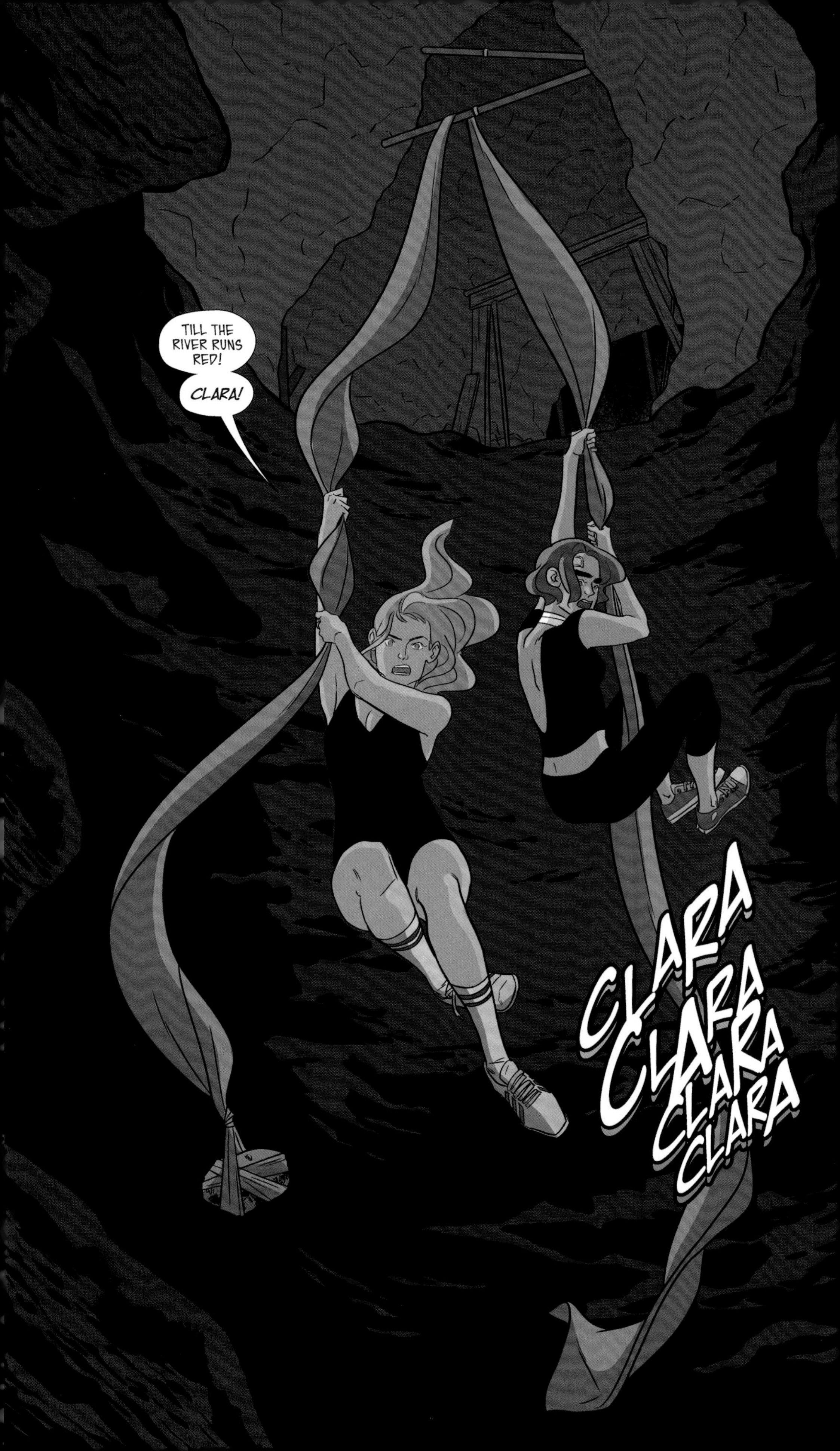
TILL THE RIVER RUNS RED!
CLARA!
CLARA CLARA CLARA CLARA

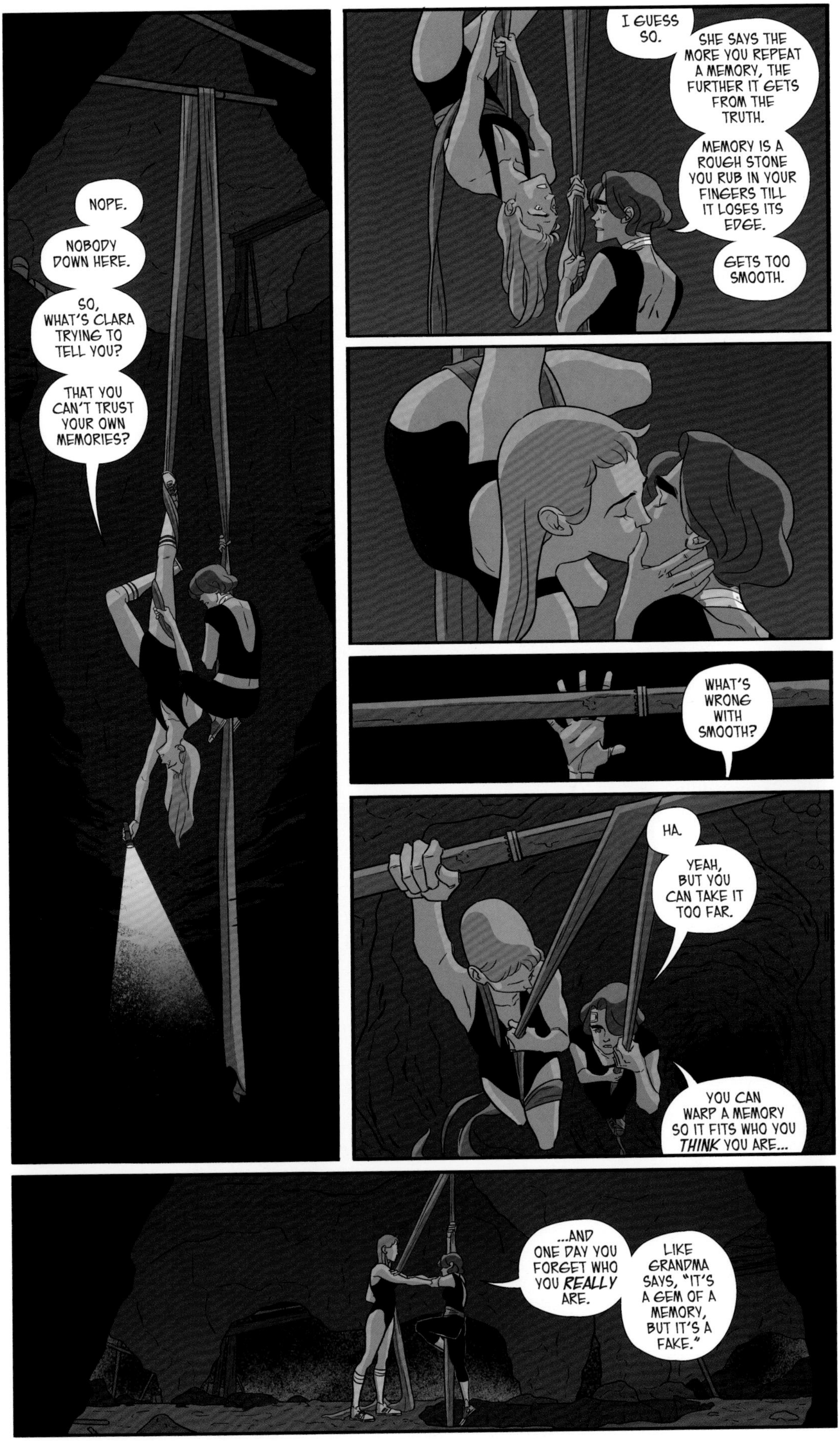
NOPE.
NOBODY DOWN HERE.
SO, WHAT'S CLARA TRYING TO TELL YOU?
THAT YOU CAN'T TRUST YOUR OWN MEMORIES?
I GUESS SO.
SHE SAYS THE MORE YOU REPEAT A MEMORY, THE FURTHER IT GETS FROM THE TRUTH.
MEMORY IS A ROUGH STONE YOU RUB IN YOUR FINGERS TILL IT LOSES ITS EDGE.
GETS TOO SMOOTH.
WHAT'S WRONG WITH SMOOTH?
HA.
YEAH, BUT YOU CAN TAKE IT TOO FAR.
YOU CAN WARP A MEMORY SO IT FITS WHO YOU *THINK* YOU ARE...
...AND ONE DAY YOU FORGET WHO YOU *REALLY* ARE.
LIKE GRANDMA SAYS, "IT'S A GEM OF A MEMORY, BUT IT'S A FAKE."

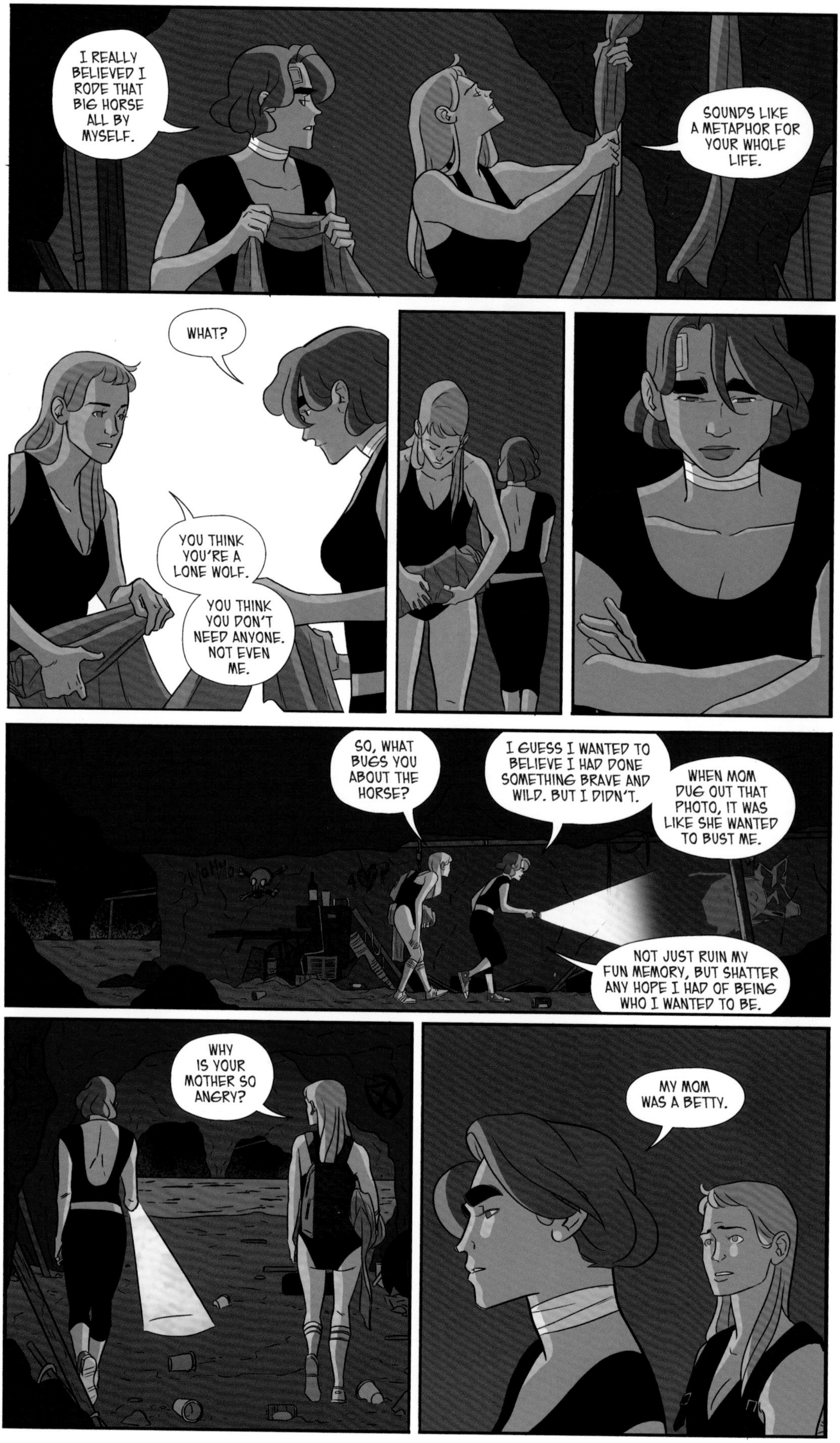
I REALLY BELIEVED I RODE THAT BIG HORSE ALL BY MYSELF.
SOUNDS LIKE A METAPHOR FOR YOUR WHOLE LIFE.
WHAT?
YOU THINK YOU'RE A LONE WOLF.
YOU THINK YOU DON'T NEED ANYONE. NOT EVEN ME.
SO, WHAT BUGS YOU ABOUT THE HORSE?
I GUESS I WANTED TO BELIEVE I HAD DONE SOMETHING BRAVE AND WILD. BUT I DIDN'T.
WHEN MOM DUG OUT THAT PHOTO, IT WAS LIKE SHE WANTED TO BUST ME.
NOT JUST RUIN MY FUN MEMORY, BUT SHATTER ANY HOPE I HAD OF BEING WHO I WANTED TO BE.
WHY IS YOUR MOTHER SO ANGRY?
MY MOM WAS A BETTY.

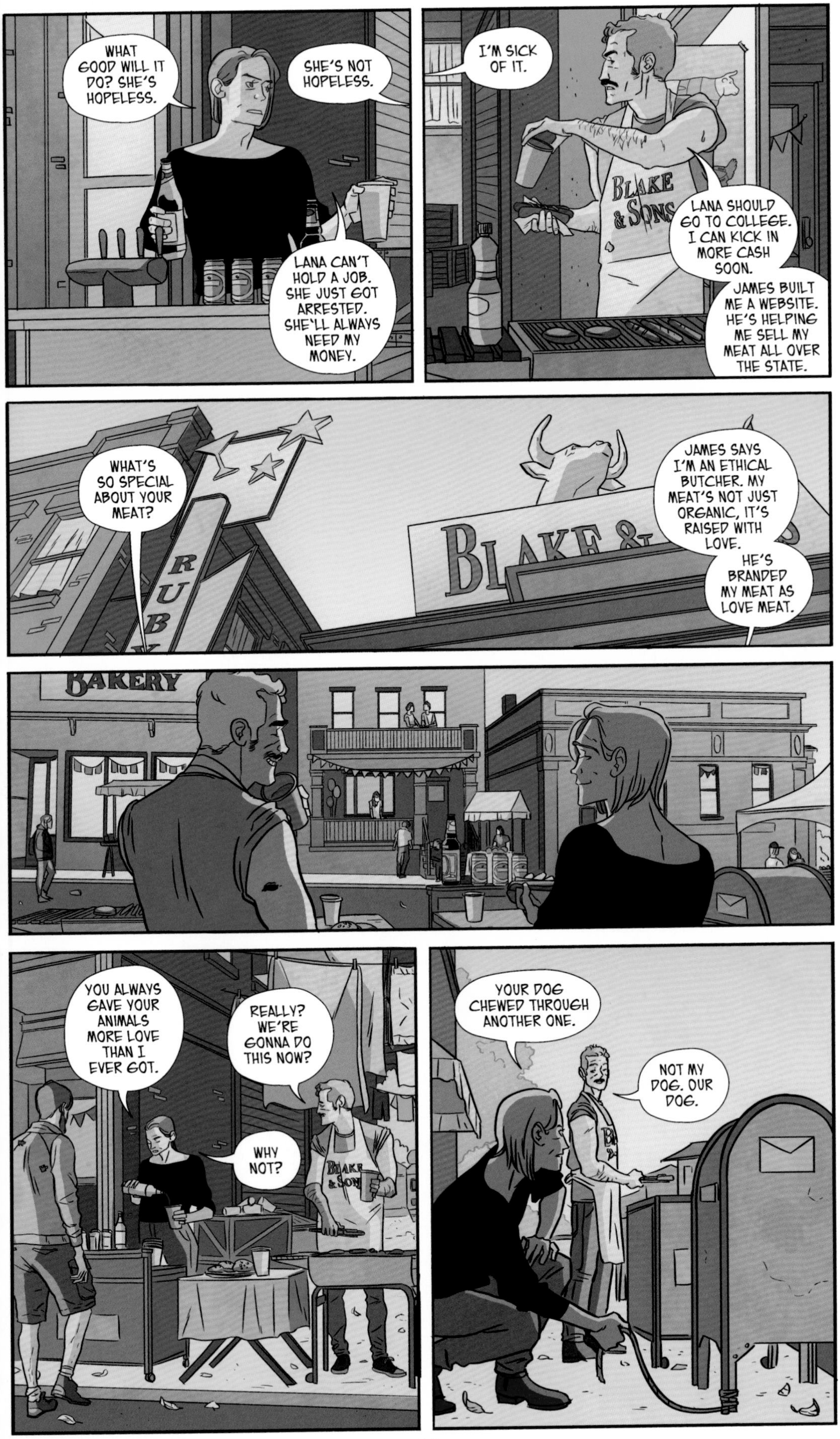
WHAT GOOD WILL IT DO? SHE'S HOPELESS.
SHE'S NOT HOPELESS.
LANA CAN'T HOLD A JOB. SHE JUST GOT ARRESTED. SHE'LL ALWAYS NEED MY MONEY.
I'M SICK OF IT.
BLAKE & SONS
LANA SHOULD GO TO COLLEGE. I CAN KICK IN MORE CASH SOON.
JAMES BUILT ME A WEBSITE. HE'S HELPING ME SELL MY MEAT ALL OVER THE STATE.
WHAT'S SO SPECIAL ABOUT YOUR MEAT?
JAMES SAYS I'M AN ETHICAL BUTCHER. MY MEAT'S NOT JUST ORGANIC, IT'S RAISED WITH LOVE.
HE'S BRANDED MY MEAT AS LOVE MEAT.
BAKERY
YOU ALWAYS GAVE YOUR ANIMALS MORE LOVE THAN I EVER GOT.
REALLY? WE'RE GONNA DO THIS NOW?
WHY NOT?
BLAKE & SONS
YOUR DOG CHEWED THROUGH ANOTHER ONE.
NOT MY DOG. OUR DOG.

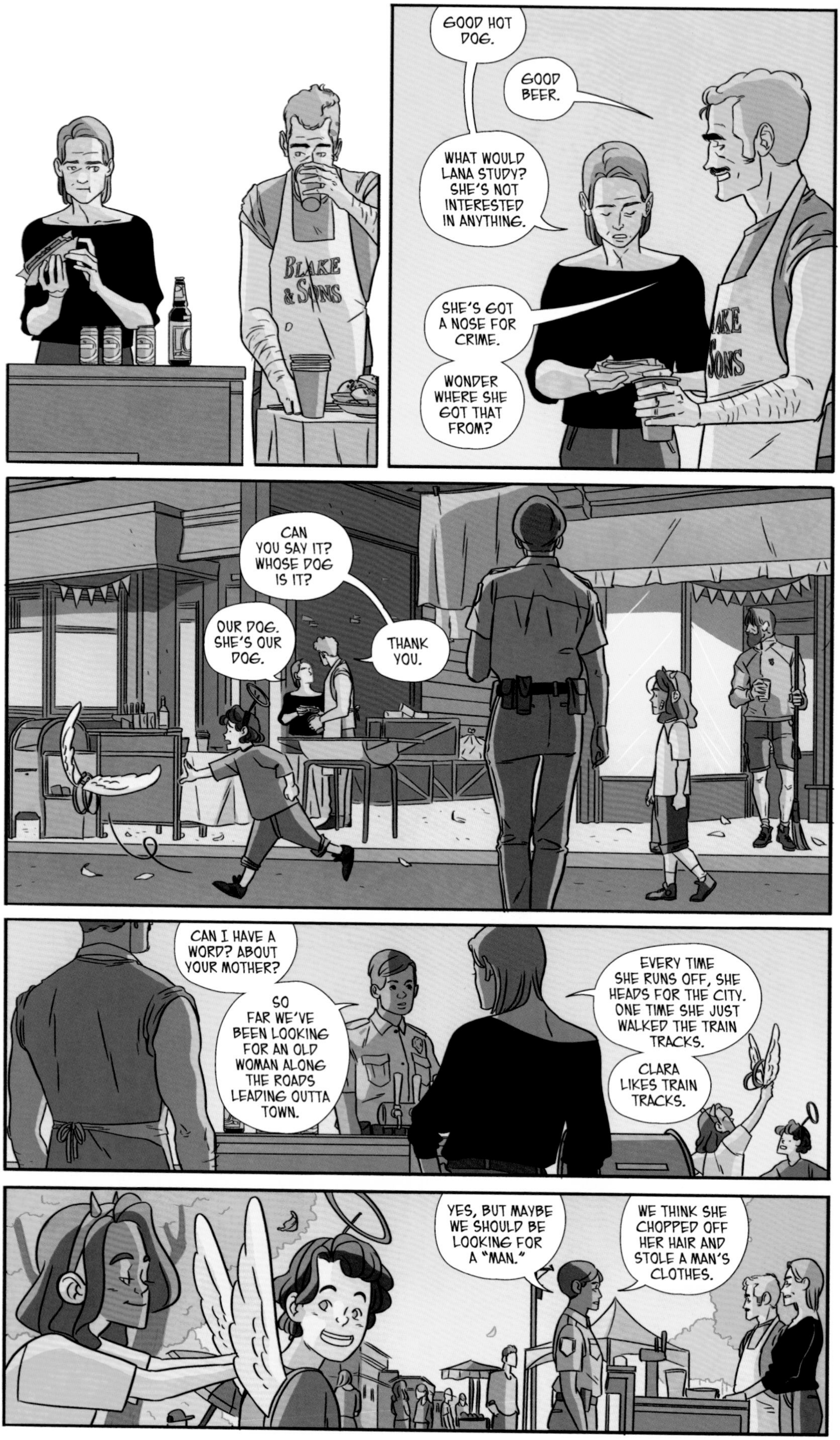

GOOD HOT DOG.
GOOD BEER.
WHAT WOULD LANA STUDY? SHE'S NOT INTERESTED IN ANYTHING.
SHE'S GOT A NOSE FOR CRIME.
WONDER WHERE SHE GOT THAT FROM?
CAN YOU SAY IT? WHOSE DOG IS IT?
OUR DOG. SHE'S OUR DOG.
THANK YOU.
CAN I HAVE A WORD? ABOUT YOUR MOTHER?
SO FAR WE'VE BEEN LOOKING FOR AN OLD WOMAN ALONG THE ROADS LEADING OUTTA TOWN.
EVERY TIME SHE RUNS OFF, SHE HEADS FOR THE CITY. ONE TIME SHE JUST WALKED THE TRAIN TRACKS.
CLARA LIKES TRAIN TRACKS.
YES, BUT MAYBE WE SHOULD BE LOOKING FOR A "MAN."
WE THINK SHE CHOPPED OFF HER HAIR AND STOLE A MAN'S CLOTHES.

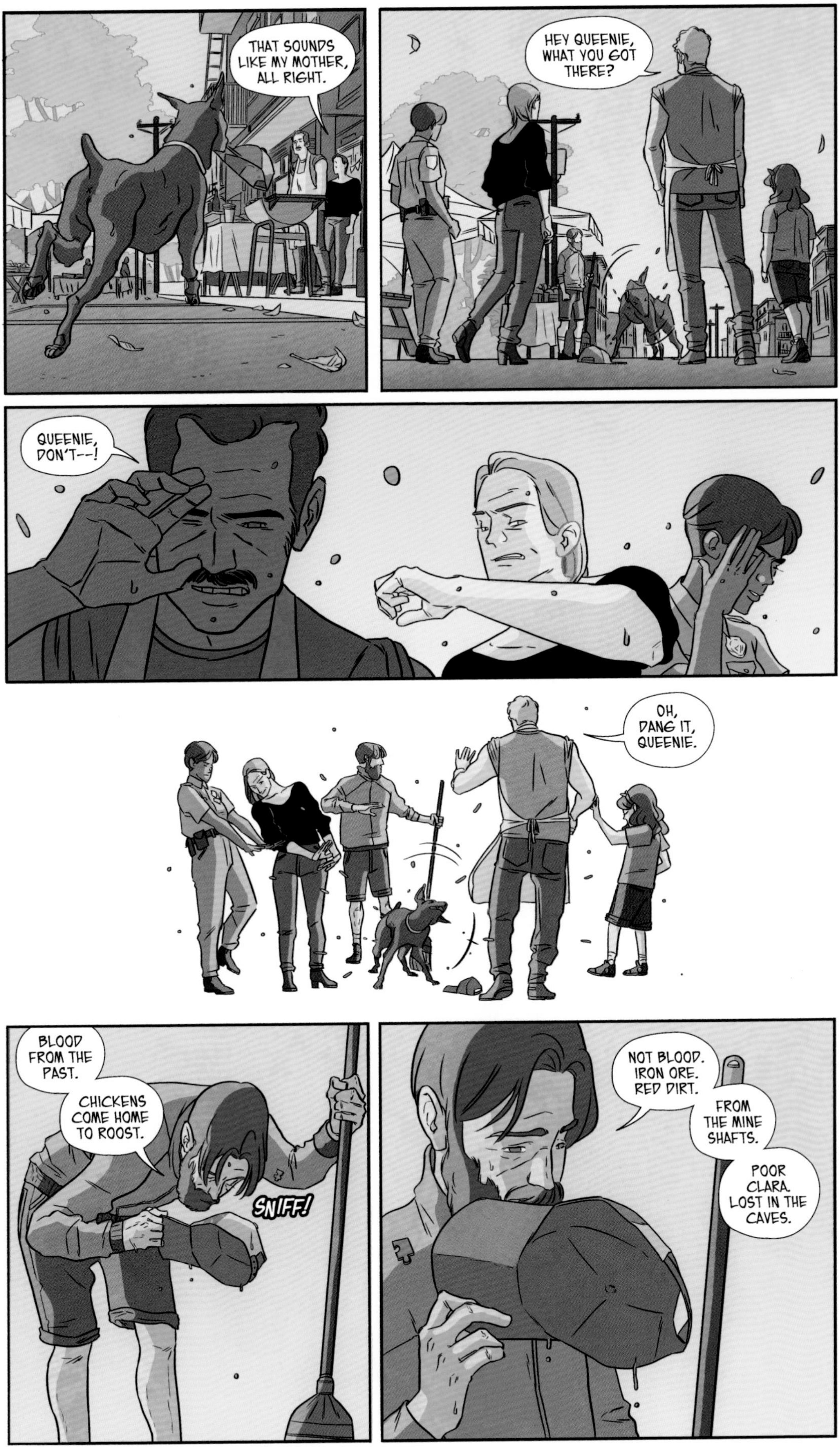

THAT SOUNDS LIKE MY MOTHER, ALL RIGHT.
HEY QUEENIE, WHAT YOU GOT THERE?
QUEENIE, DON'T--!
OH, DANG IT, QUEENIE.
BLOOD FROM THE PAST.
CHICKENS COME HOME TO ROOST.
SNIFF!
NOT BLOOD. IRON ORE. RED DIRT.
FROM THE MINE SHAFTS.
POOR CLARA. LOST IN THE CAVES.

WHAT DO YOU MEAN, YOUR MOM WAS A BETTY?

BETTY WAS PROGRESSIVE. A LIBERATED WOMAN, AHEAD OF HER TIMES.

WELL, THAT'S WHAT THEY SAY, ANYWAY. THAT'S THE LEGEND.

MAYBE IT'S ALL BULLSHIT. A MYTH.

DADDY SAID MY MOM WAS LIKE HER.

SHE WANTED TO SPLIT RUBY FALLS AND TRY HER LUCK IN THE BIG CITY. LEAVE SMALL-TOWN HELL.

SO WHAT STOPPED HER?

ME.

SHE GOT PREGNANT. SHE HAD TO STAY IN THE BAR AND SLING DRINKS.

SOME FATE, HUH? SLOW DEATH, COCKTAIL BY COCKTAIL.

I'M HER BALL AND CHAIN. I WRECKED HER LIFE.

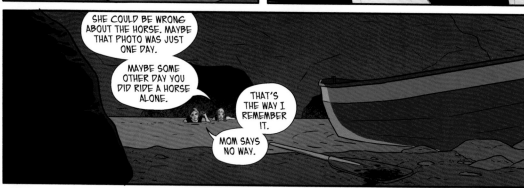

SHE COULD BE WRONG ABOUT THE HORSE. MAYBE THAT PHOTO WAS JUST ONE DAY.

MAYBE SOME OTHER DAY YOU DID RIDE A HORSE ALONE.

THAT'S THE WAY I REMEMBER IT.

MOM SAYS NO WAY.

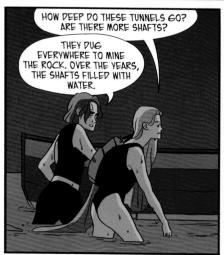

HOW DEEP DO THESE TUNNELS GO? ARE THERE MORE SHAFTS?

THEY DUG EVERYWHERE TO MINE THE ROCK. OVER THE YEARS, THE SHAFTS FILLED WITH WATER.

EASY TO GET LOST IN HERE.

IS THAT BLOOD?

GRANDMA!

OVER HERE!

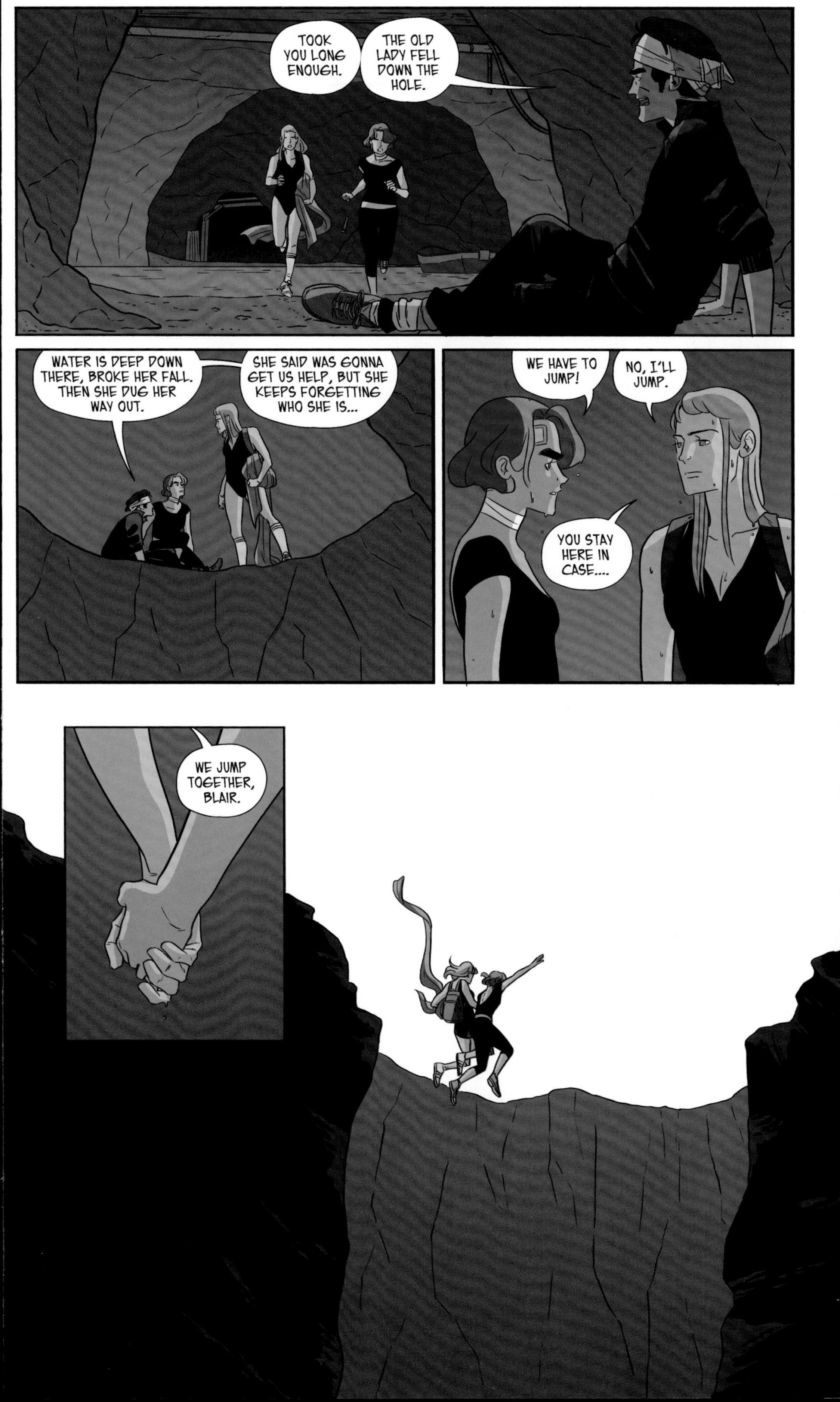
TOOK YOU LONG ENOUGH.
THE OLD LADY FELL DOWN THE HOLE.
WATER IS DEEP DOWN THERE, BROKE HER FALL. THEN SHE DUG HER WAY OUT.
SHE SAID WAS GONNA GET US HELP, BUT SHE KEEPS FORGETTING WHO SHE IS...
WE HAVE TO JUMP!
NO, I'LL JUMP.
YOU STAY HERE IN CASE....
WE JUMP TOGETHER, BLAIR.

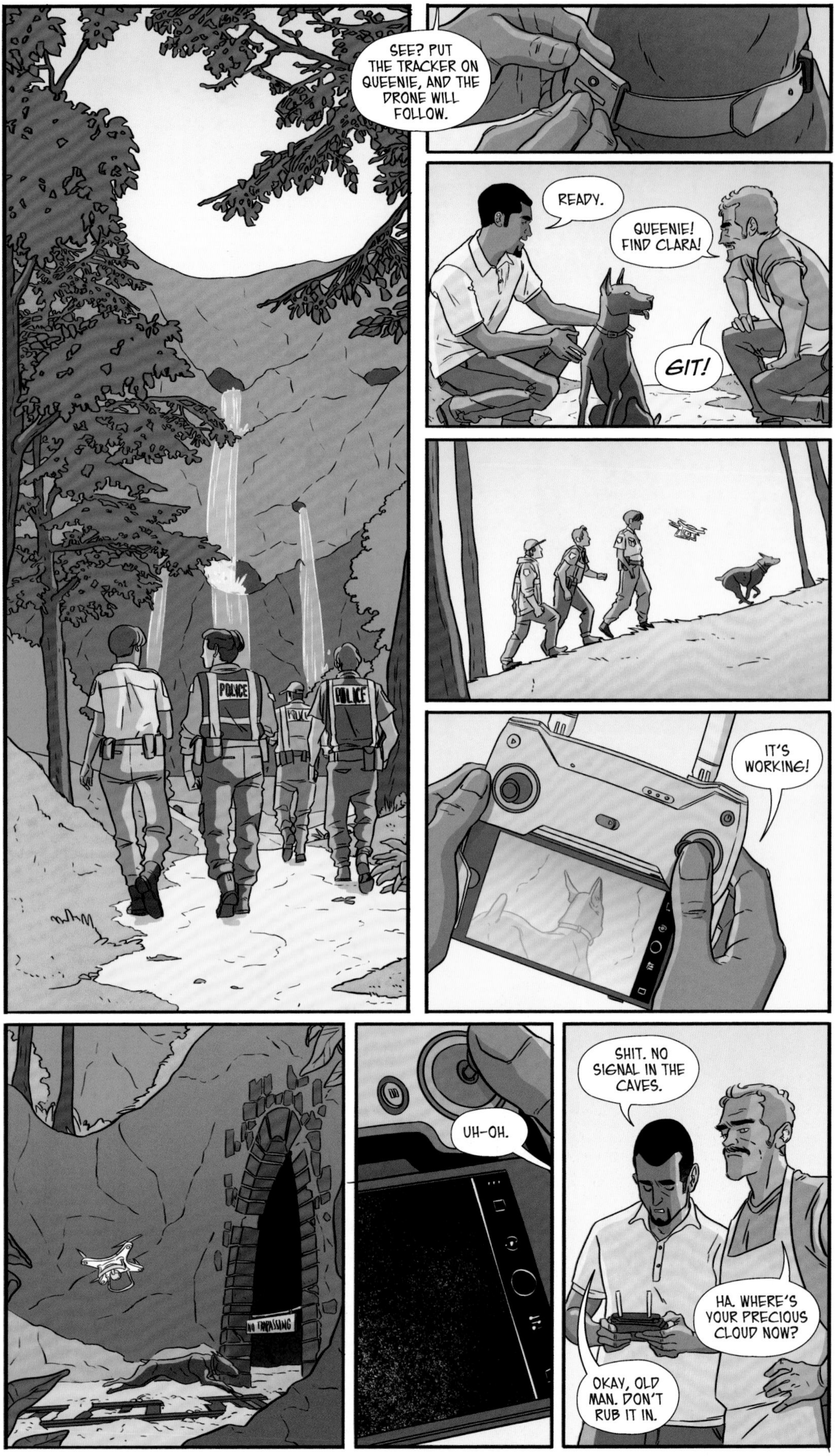
SEE? PUT THE TRACKER ON QUEENIE, AND THE DRONE WILL FOLLOW.
POLICE
POLICE
POLICE
READY.
QUEENIE! FIND CLARA!
GIT!
IT'S WORKING!
NO TRESPASSING
UH-OH.
SHIT. NO SIGNAL IN THE CAVES.
HA. WHERE'S YOUR PRECIOUS CLOUD NOW?
OKAY, OLD MAN. DON'T RUB IT IN.

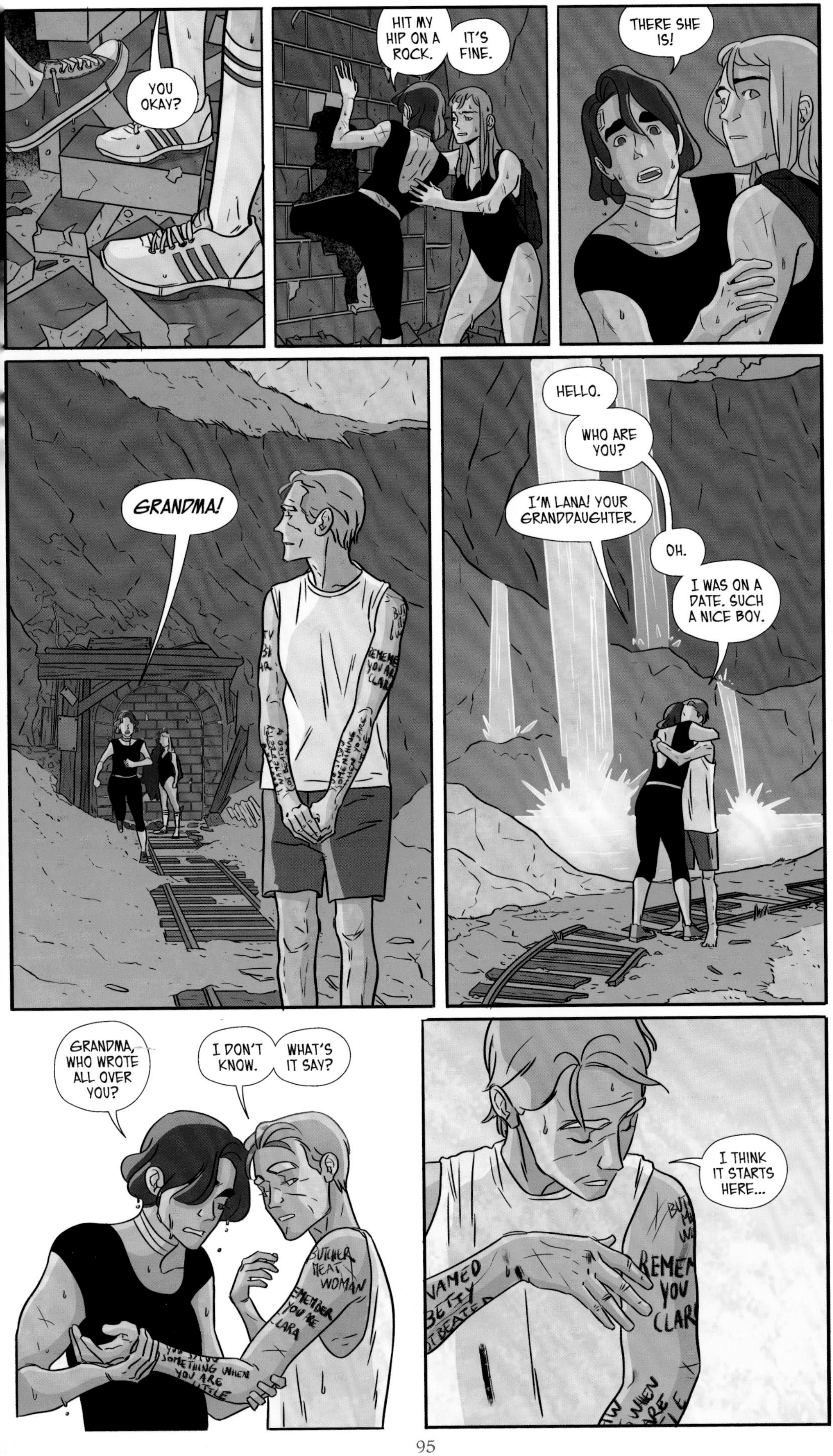
YOU OKAY?
HIT MY HIP ON A ROCK.
IT'S FINE.
THERE SHE IS!
GRANDMA!
HELLO.
WHO ARE YOU?
I'M LANA! YOUR GRANDDAUGHTER.
OH.
I WAS ON A DATE. SUCH A NICE BOY.
GRANDMA, WHO WROTE ALL OVER YOU?
I DON'T KNOW.
WHAT'S IT SAY?
I THINK IT STARTS HERE...

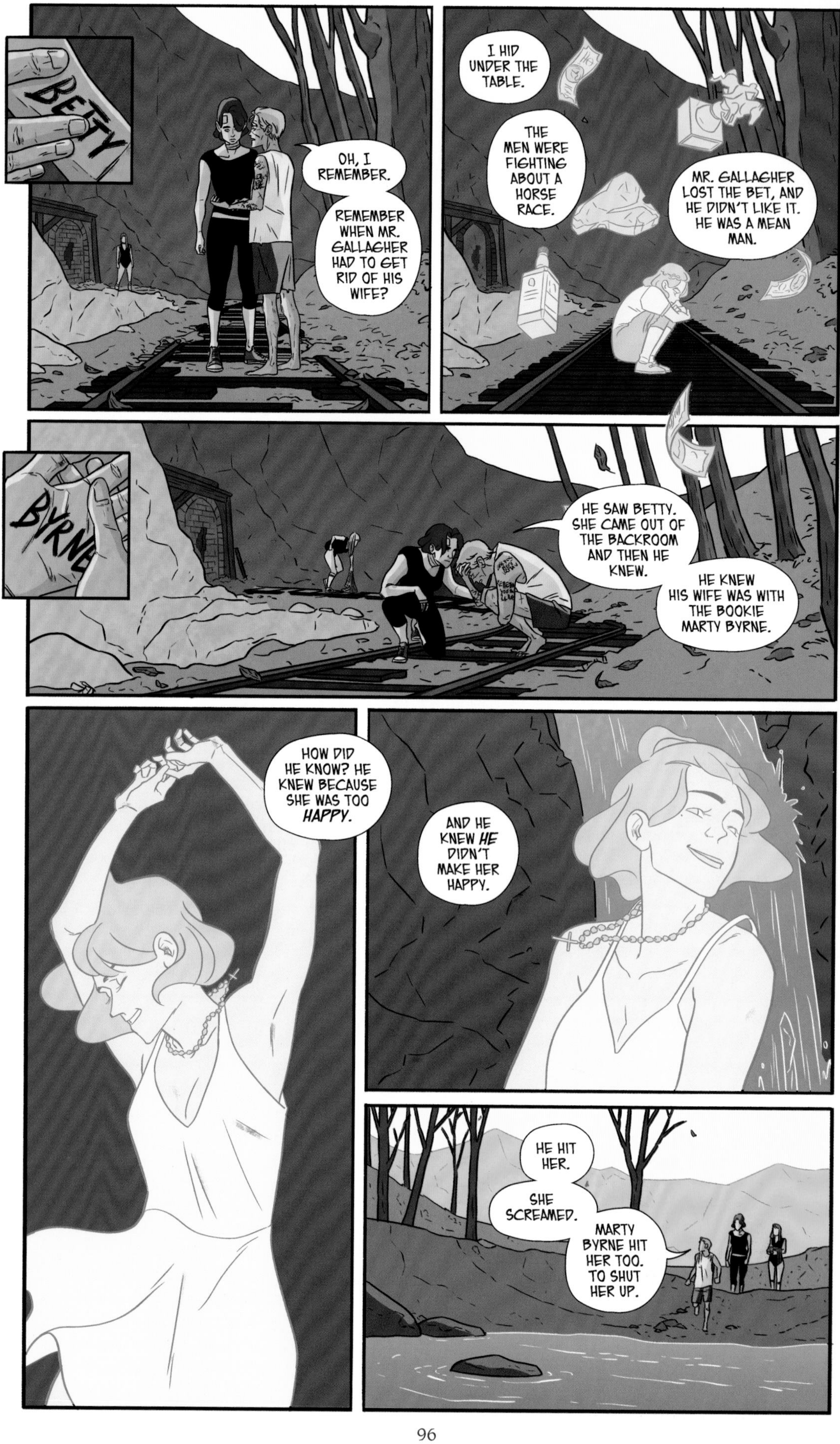
BETTY
OH, I REMEMBER.
REMEMBER WHEN MR. GALLAGHER HAD TO GET RID OF HIS WIFE?
I HID UNDER THE TABLE.
THE MEN WERE FIGHTING ABOUT A HORSE RACE.
MR. GALLAGHER LOST THE BET, AND HE DIDN'T LIKE IT. HE WAS A MEAN MAN.
BYRNE
HE SAW BETTY. SHE CAME OUT OF THE BACKROOM AND THEN HE KNEW.
HE KNEW HIS WIFE WAS WITH THE BOOKIE MARTY BYRNE.
HOW DID HE KNOW? HE KNEW BECAUSE SHE WAS TOO *HAPPY*.
AND HE KNEW *HE* DIDN'T MAKE HER HAPPY.
HE HIT HER.
SHE SCREAMED.
MARTY BYRNE HIT HER TOO. TO SHUT HER UP.

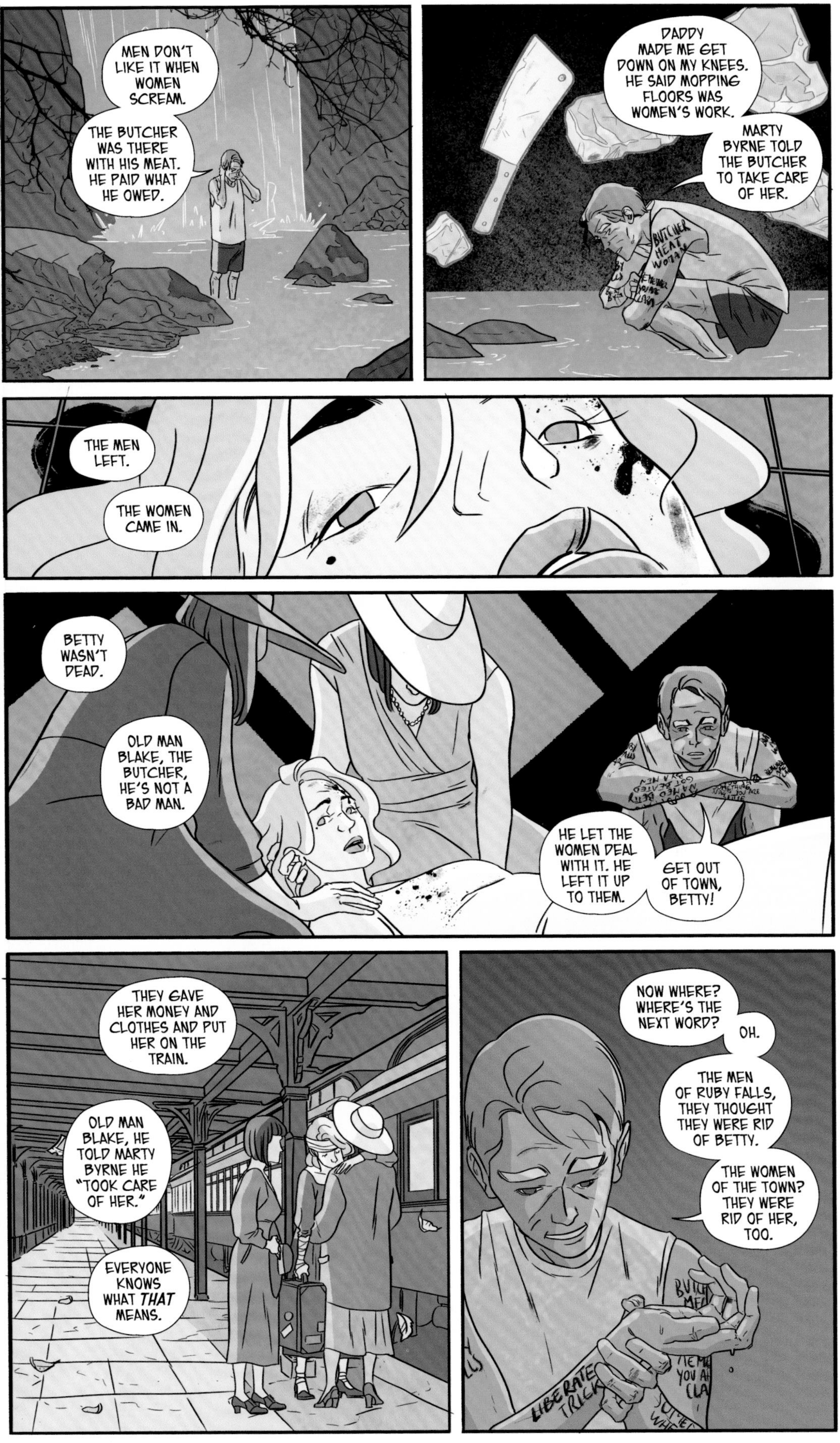
MEN DON'T LIKE IT WHEN WOMEN SCREAM.
THE BUTCHER WAS THERE WITH HIS MEAT. HE PAID WHAT HE OWED.
DADDY MADE ME GET DOWN ON MY KNEES. HE SAID MOPPING FLOORS WAS WOMEN'S WORK.
MARTY BYRNE TOLD THE BUTCHER TO TAKE CARE OF HER.
THE MEN LEFT.
THE WOMEN CAME IN.
BETTY WASN'T DEAD.
OLD MAN BLAKE, THE BUTCHER, HE'S NOT A BAD MAN.
HE LET THE WOMEN DEAL WITH IT. HE LEFT IT UP TO THEM.
GET OUT OF TOWN, BETTY!
THEY GAVE HER MONEY AND CLOTHES AND PUT HER ON THE TRAIN.
OLD MAN BLAKE, HE TOLD MARTY BYRNE HE "TOOK CARE OF HER."
EVERYONE KNOWS WHAT *THAT* MEANS.
NOW WHERE? WHERE'S THE NEXT WORD?
OH.
THE MEN OF RUBY FALLS, THEY THOUGHT THEY WERE RID OF BETTY.
THE WOMEN OF THE TOWN? THEY WERE RID OF HER, TOO.
LIBERATE TRICK

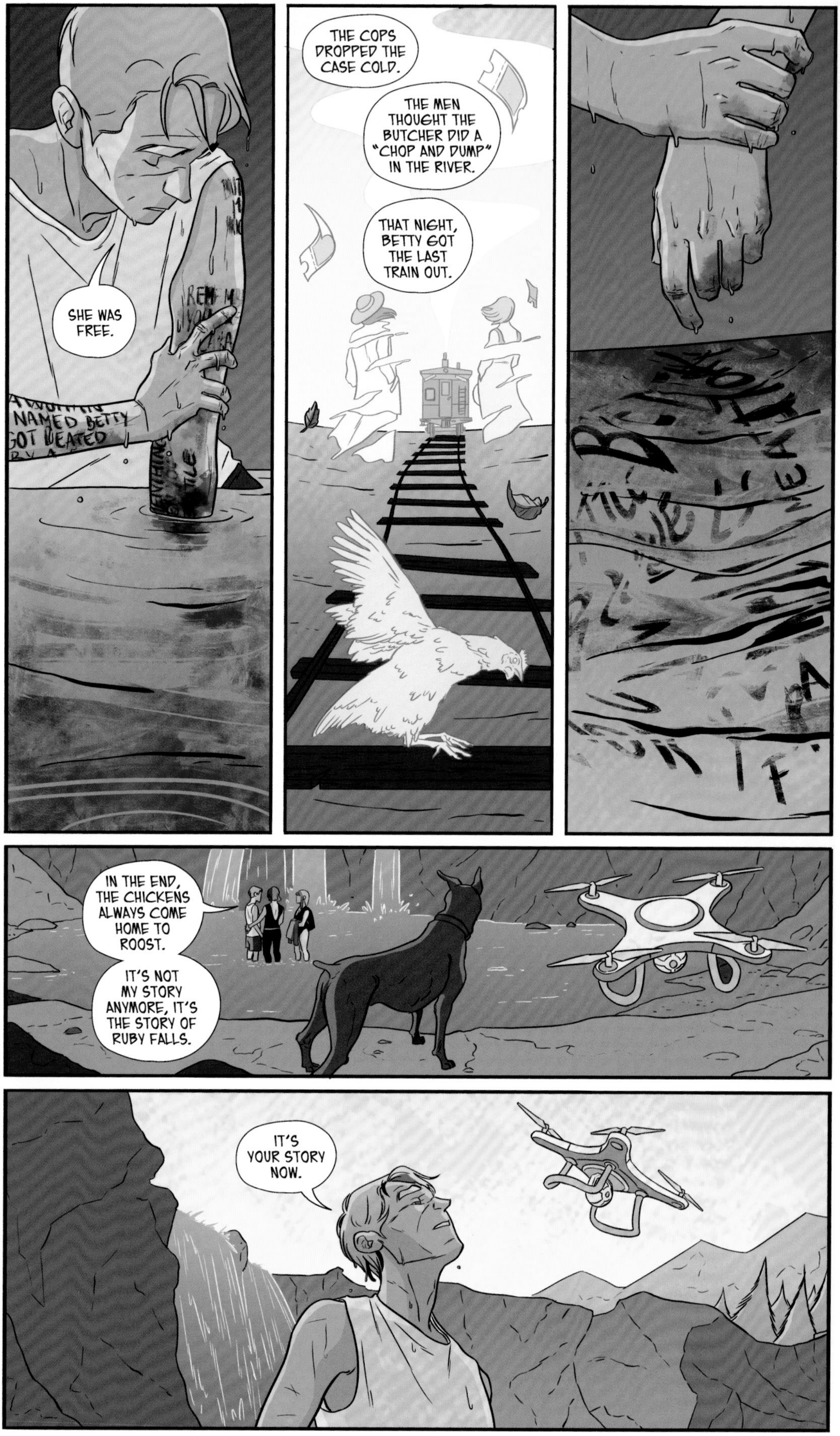
SHE WAS FREE.
THE COPS DROPPED THE CASE COLD.
THE MEN THOUGHT THE BUTCHER DID A "CHOP AND DUMP" IN THE RIVER.
THAT NIGHT, BETTY GOT THE LAST TRAIN OUT.
IN THE END, THE CHICKENS ALWAYS COME HOME TO ROOST.
IT'S NOT MY STORY ANYMORE, IT'S THE STORY OF RUBY FALLS.
IT'S YOUR STORY NOW.

ENOUGH OF THIS "MEN ONLY" CRAP.

I'M BUYING THESE LADIES A DRINK.

BREAK THE LAWS THAT ARE WRONG, I SAY.

MOM!

LET HER TALK IT OUT. SHE NEEDS THIS.

YOU WOMEN HAVE IT TOUGHER THAN US MEN. SO I'M BUYIN'.

LINE 'EM UP, BARTENDER.

DADDY KEEPS THE WHISKEY STILL IN THE CHICKEN COOP.

CHICKENS GET DRUNK ON FUMES.

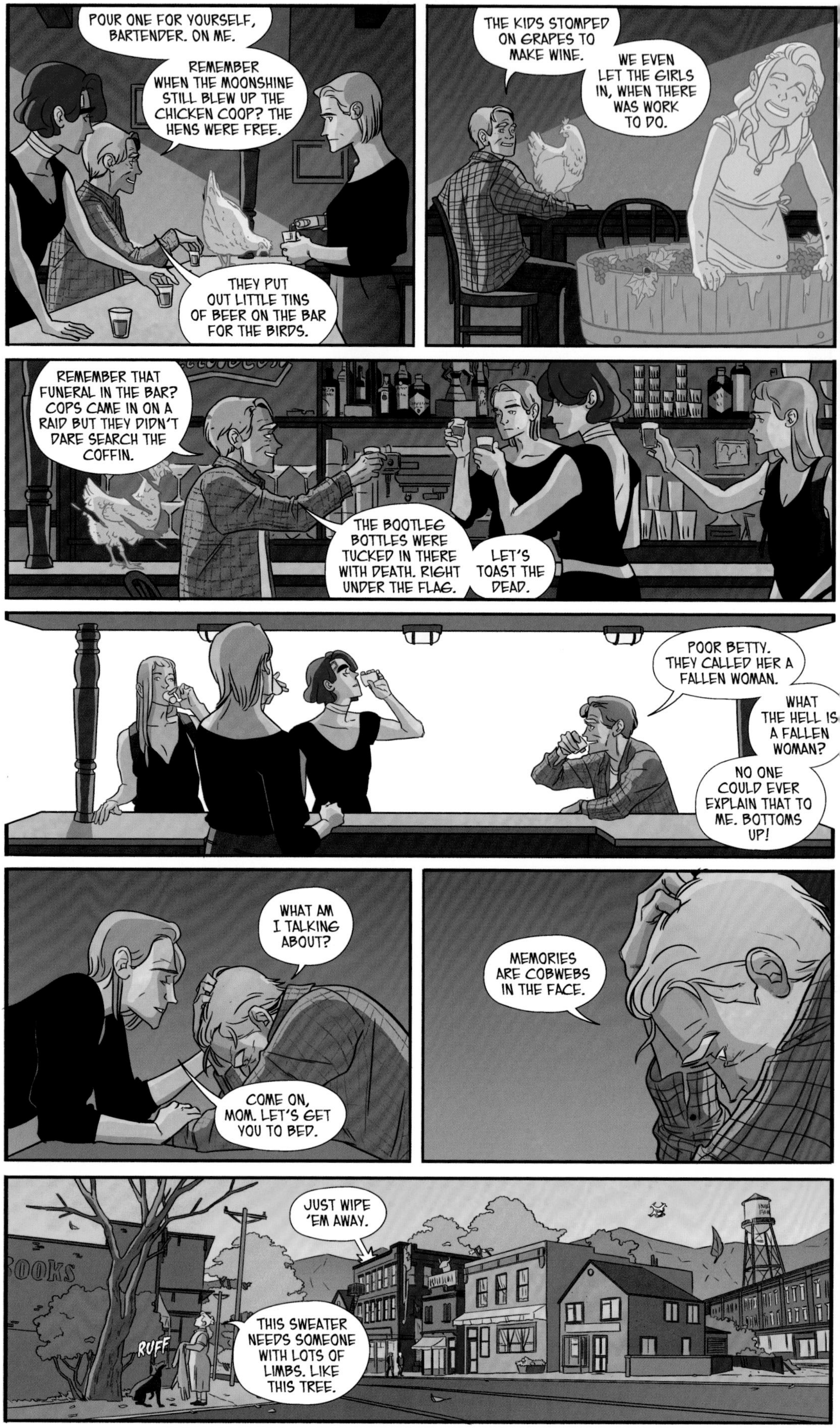
POUR ONE FOR YOURSELF, BARTENDER. ON ME.
REMEMBER WHEN THE MOONSHINE STILL BLEW UP THE CHICKEN COOP? THE HENS WERE FREE.
THEY PUT OUT LITTLE TINS OF BEER ON THE BAR FOR THE BIRDS.
THE KIDS STOMPED ON GRAPES TO MAKE WINE.
WE EVEN LET THE GIRLS IN, WHEN THERE WAS WORK TO DO.
REMEMBER THAT FUNERAL IN THE BAR? COPS CAME IN ON A RAID BUT THEY DIDN'T DARE SEARCH THE COFFIN.
THE BOOTLEG BOTTLES WERE TUCKED IN THERE WITH DEATH. RIGHT UNDER THE FLAG.
LET'S TOAST THE DEAD.
POOR BETTY. THEY CALLED HER A FALLEN WOMAN.
WHAT THE HELL IS A FALLEN WOMAN?
NO ONE COULD EVER EXPLAIN THAT TO ME. BOTTOMS UP!
WHAT AM I TALKING ABOUT?
COME ON, MOM. LET'S GET YOU TO BED.
MEMORIES ARE COBWEBS IN THE FACE.
JUST WIPE 'EM AWAY.
BOOKS
RUFF
THIS SWEATER NEEDS SOMEONE WITH LOTS OF LIMBS. LIKE THIS TREE.

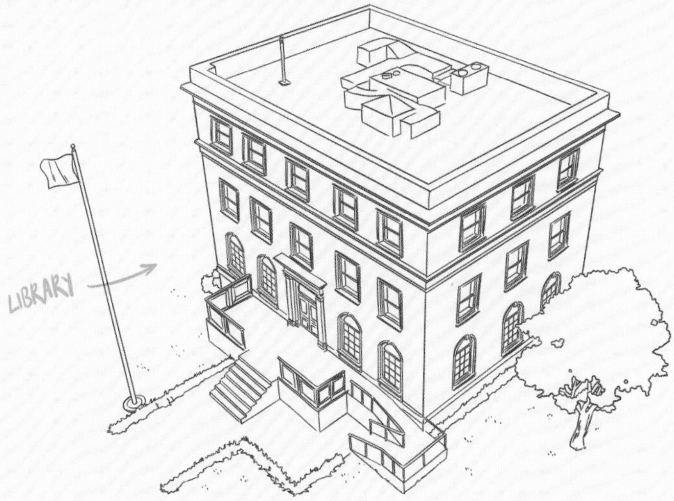
LIBRARY

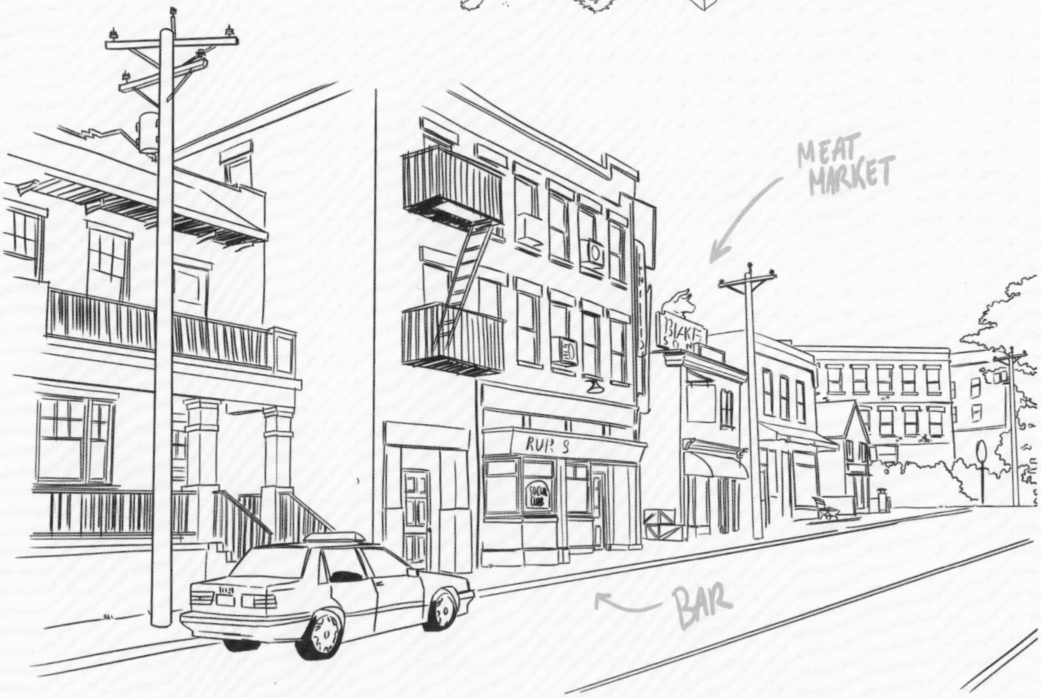
MEAT MARKET
SOCIAL CLUB
BAR

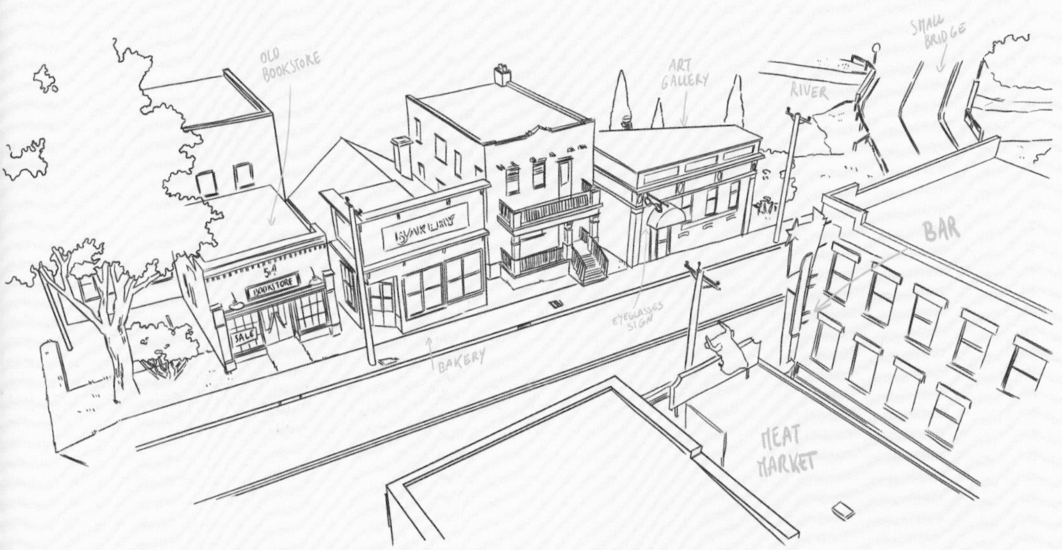
OLD BOOKSTORE
ART GALLERY
RIVER
SMALL BRIDGE
BOOKSTORE
SALE
BAKERY
EYEGLASSES SIGN
BAR
MEAT MARKET

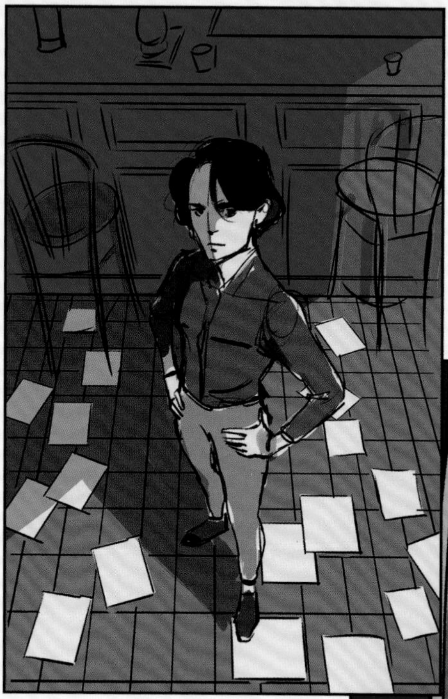

alternate cover designs

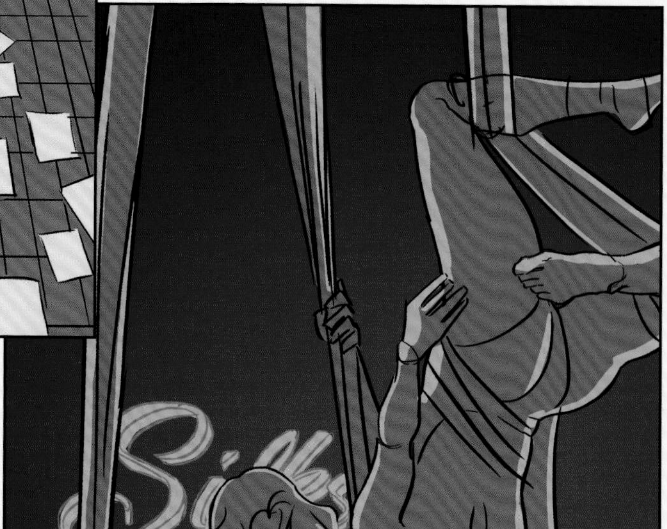

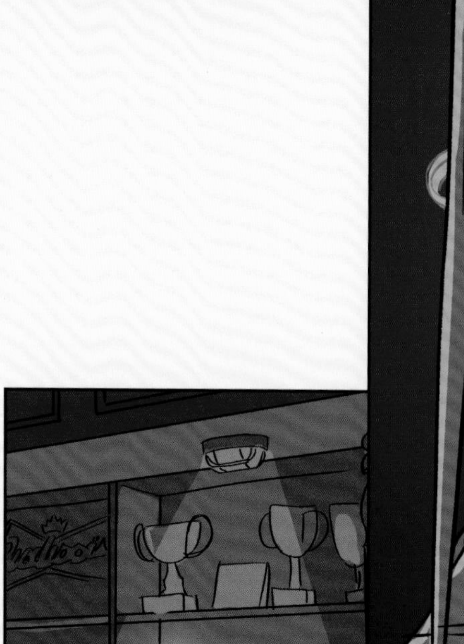

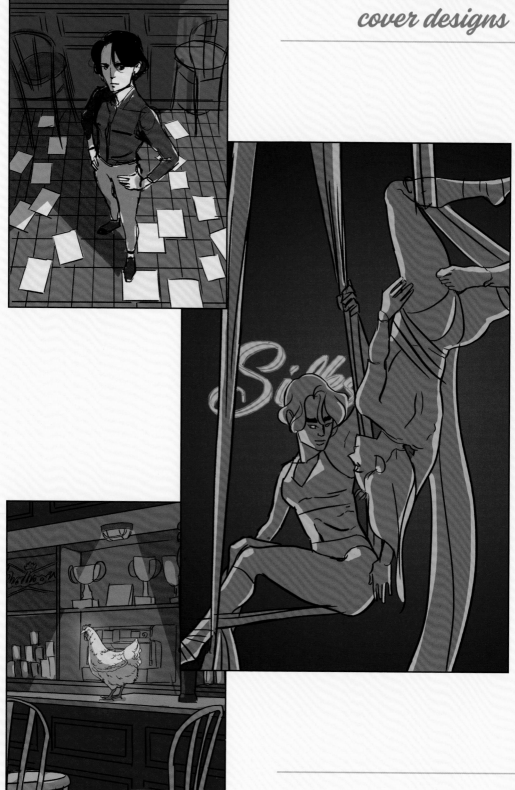

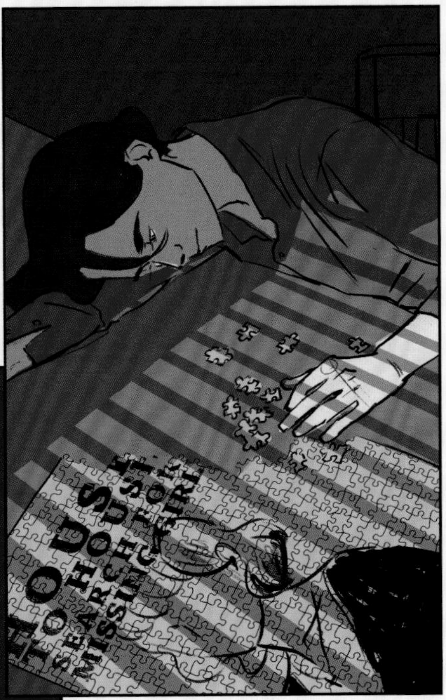
HOUSE
TO HOUSE
SEARCH FOR
MISSING GIRL

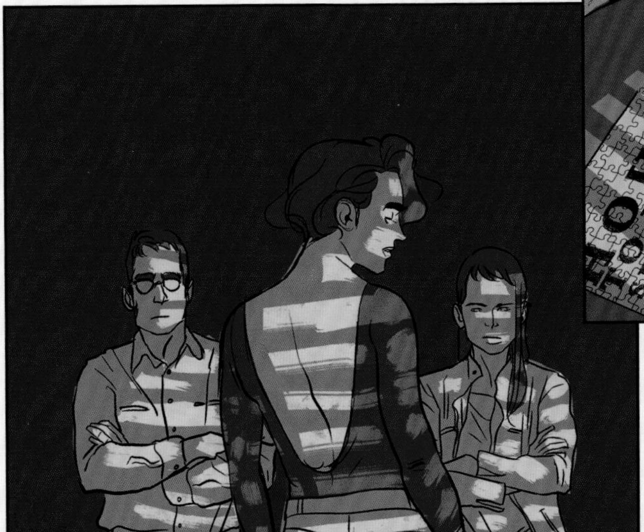

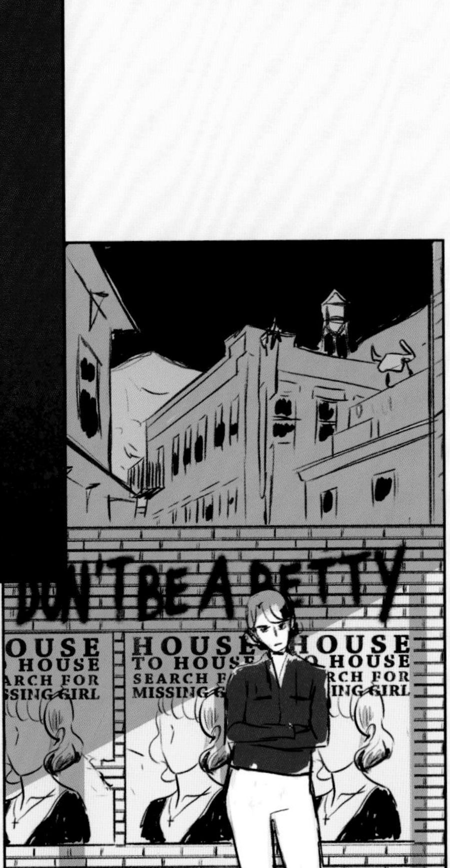
DON'T BE A BETTY
HOUSE
TO HOUSE
SEARCH FOR
MISSING GIRL
HOUSE
TO HOUSE
SEARCH F
MISSING G
HOUSE
O HOUSE
ARCH FOR
SING GIRL

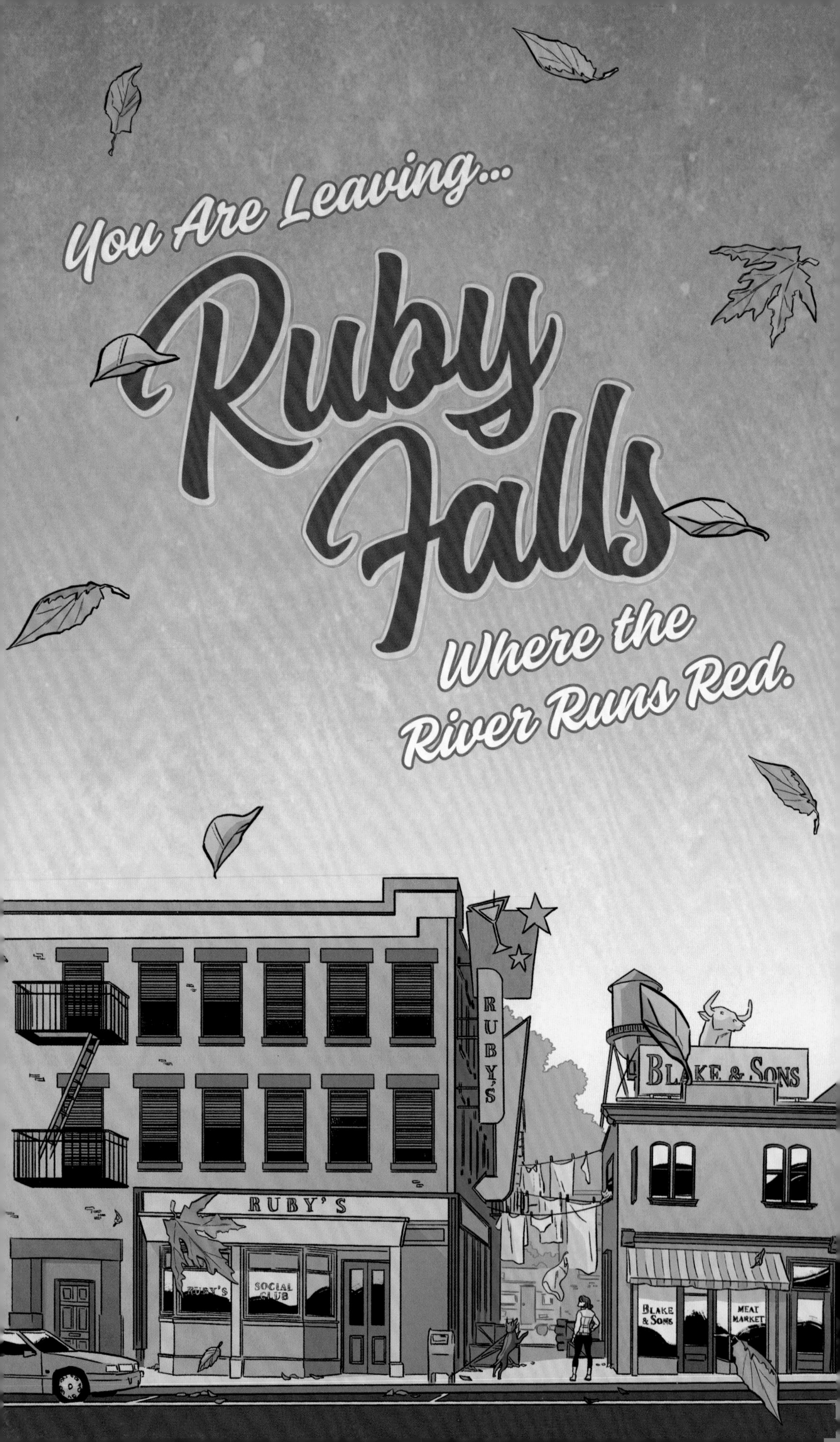
You Are Leaving...
Ruby Falls
Where the River Runs Red.
RUBY'S
BLAKE & SONS
RUBY'S
RUBY'S
SOCIAL CLUB
BLAKE & SONS
MEAT MARKET